"Each day's headlines demonstrate the timeliness of this important analysis of the emerging transnational radical Islamic movement. Of particular interest is Dennis' call for a United States missile defense capability to deal with the distinct --and growing-- danger that extremist Islamic elements may seek to exploit our present vulnerability to missile attack with devastating results."

Frank Gaffney, Former Assistant
Secretary of Defense for International
Security under President Reagan

The Rise of the Islamic Empire and the Threat to the West

Anthony J. Dennis

Wyndham Hall Press

THE RISE OF THE ISLAMIC EMPIRE
and the THREAT TO THE WEST

By ANTHONY J. DENNIS

Copyright © 1996 by Anthony J. Dennis

Second Edition
ISBN: 1-55605-339-8

Publisher's Cataloging in Publication

Dennis, Anthony J.
   The rise of the Islamic empire and the threat to the
West / Anthony J. Dennis
      p. cm.
   Pre-assigned LCCN: 96-60512
   Includes bibliographic references
   ISBN 1-55605-267-7
   ISBN 1-55605-268-5

Wyndham Hall Press
Lima, Ohio 45806

Printed in The United States of America

Turning and turning in the widening gyre
The falcon cannot hear the falconer;
Things fall apart; the centre cannot hold;
Mere anarchy is loosed upon the world...

-excerpt from "The Second Coming"
by William Butler Yeats[1].

Endnote: 1. Yeats, "The Second Coming," 91.

SECOND EDITION FOREWORD

The public's interest in the goals and ideology of the transnational Muslim fundamentalist movement has increased dramatically since the September 11th terrorist attacks against the United States. This book provides a helpful description of this deadly movement and the political dynamic and "mindset" which fuels it. In these pages you will find a capsule history of Islam and the reasons why, unlike most religions, Islam concerns itself not only with spiritual questions but also political ones. From the very start, Islam has represented a total way of life for its adherents, governing not only individual practice and belief but also ordering the social and political structure of Islamic society and even directing the nature and course of Islam's relations with non-Muslim peoples and nations.

When I first wrote an analysis and description of the Muslim fundamentalist movement and advanced the thesis that these groups (as distinguished from all of Islam) represented a "threat to the West," the world as we know it had not yet come into being. Sadly, the terrorist threat I had predicted has now become a reality. As a consequence, this volume has become all the more relevant, and its recommendations for protecting Americans at home and abroad are all the more urgent.

September 11th is only "chapter one" in what promises to be a long battle with a movement that perceives America and the West as "infidels" who must be converted or destroyed.

We must continue to be vigilant. And we must continue to understand the objectives and radically different world view that these groups possess, or else we risk a repeat of September 11th.

Anthony J. Dennis
November 18, 2001

FOREWORD

Islam in its current crusading form (often called "fundamentalist") is more than a religion today, it is a worldwide revolutionary movement[1]. As such, it deserves to be seriously studied and debated from a secular perspective as a revolutionary ideology. Is this ideology avowedly hostile or friendly to the non-Muslim world? What does this ideology mean for the safety and security of the West? Depending on the answers to the above questions, what policies should Western governments adopt in order to fulfill their basic obligation to protect their citizenry from bodily harm?

Islam is one of the great religions of the world. Its tenets of peace, mercy, charity toward those less fortunate, respect for life and longstanding tradition of tolerance toward those of other faiths are qualities to be universally admired. The world would indeed be a better place in many respects if more members of the world community used the Koran or other holy works such as the Bible as the touchstone for their public and private actions.

But Islam more recently has been used in a cynical and calculated fashion by ruthless dictators and politicians seeking to wield political power in their own countries and abroad. The social and economic conditions found within much of the Muslim world favor leaders like the fundamentalists who are able to capitalize on feelings of anger, helplessness and rage[2]. Much of the populace found in the Middle East, Central Asia and northern Africa is inordinately young, uneducated and desperately poor[3]. With the advent of satellite dishes and mass telecommunications these people are acutely aware of their own poverty and all too familiar with the wealth and easy lifestyle enjoyed by the Western world. No wonder then that they are left with a sense that the world has passed them by. This is a dangerous combination for the current crop of secular leaders and a golden opportunity for those seeking to seize power.

And what would an Islamic dictatorship look like? The widespread torture, repression, killing and other acts of violence committed on an ongoing basis by such avowedly Islamic dictatorships as currently exist in Iran and Sudan are well known. The criminal acts and systematic human rights abuses committed by these governments have been thoroughly documented by the United Nations Commission on Human Rights, Amnesty International, the world press and other groups. Furthermore, the words and deeds of radical Islamic activists throughout the world constitute additional proof that the religious dictatorships the fundamentalists seek to bring to power in still more areas of the world would undoubtedly be violent, repressive toward their own people and openly hostile toward the West. The killing of innocent tourists in Egypt by Muslim activists, most likely members of the Muslim Brotherhood or *Jamaat al-Jihad* (the Organization for Holy War), and the sentencing to death of British citizen and author Salman Rushdie by Iran's Ayatollah Khomeini in February, 1989 for exercising his basic human right to freedom of intellectual expression should give every civilized member of the world community, Muslim and non-Muslim alike, cause for concern.

This author believes in an equal and balanced treatment of both the Muslim and non-Muslim worlds. Islam no more compels the murder of innocent tourists in Egypt or the murder and mayhem expressly committed in the name of Islam by terrorists in New York City than the Bible compelled the sack of Jerusalem and the slaughter of many of that city's inhabitants by the Western Crusaders in 1099 AD. All of these actions should be equally and roundly condemned.

There are dangerous forces at work in the world today, unleashed largely by the death of another worldwide ideology that captured the imagination of so many people throughout the world: Communism. History teaches us that the power vacuum that now exists in Central Asia and parts of Africa and the Middle East as a result of the collapse of the Soviet Empire will not go unfilled for long. Iranian agents, under the direction and control of foreign minister Ali Akbar Velayati and others, are already hard at work building military, political and economic alliances with the newly independent Central Asian Muslim countries. Throughout the Middle East, North Africa and Asia, Islam has influenced and altered the very vocabulary of the political debate. Fundamentalist Islam has already become the new language of political conflict and control in many parts of the world. It is the thesis of this work that Islam in its violent, reactionary, fundamentalist form will constitute the number one threat to world peace and the very survival of the human species in the late 1990s and beyond. Viewed in historical terms, the worldwide radical Islamic revolution of the late 20th century has only just begun.

It is indeed unfortunate that the expanding world of radical, Islamic fundamentalism and the Western world (comprising for purposes of this study North America, Europe, Israel and, politically and industrially at least, Japan) seem to be on a collision course on many different levels both cultural and political. This work was written in the hope that citizens and policy makers in the West will recognize the new and dangerous trajectory the world is on and make provisions for all possible diplomatic and military contingencies while there is still time. With the end of the Cold War, there is a widespread tendency to bury our collective heads in the sand and take a well deserved nap. Now is not the time for napping.

Anthony J. Dennis

§ § §

ENDNOTES

1. Daniel Pipes, editor of the *Middle East Quarterly*, has characterized fundamentalist Islam as "a radical utopian ideology." See Winkler, "Islam and Democracy," A10.

2. Phillips, "The Saddamization of Iran," 6,7,10.

3. Ibid. See also Hovsepian, "Competing Ideologies in the Arab World," p. 22.

ACKNOWLEDGMENTS

There were many people whose comments, suggestions, insights and moral support contributed to the successful completion of this book. In particular, I would like to thank Dr. Daniel Pipes, Editor of the *Middle East Quarterly* and Director of the Middle East Forum, for his helpful comments on an earlier draft; Ambassador Henry F. Cooper for his cooperation throughout; Professor Leila Fawaz, chairperson of the Tufts University history department and an eminent Middle East historian in her own right; Professor Tony Smith of the Tufts University political science department for leading me to Ernest Gellner's writings; former U.S. Ambassador to the Soviet Union Malcolm Toon for his encouragement and helpful critique of an earlier draft; Dr. Brice Cassenti of the United Technologies Research Center, for his technical expertise, comments and suggestions concerning my treatment of the Manhattan Project, SDI and ballistic missile defense systems; Congresswoman Nancy L. Johnson (R-CT) and members of her staff; Senator Joseph Lieberman (D-CT) and his staff; the American Security Council Foundation located in Washington, D.C. for granting me access to otherwise unreachable sources; international business consultant and Fletcher School of Law and Diplomacy graduate Mark Ferri of Boston, Massachusetts; and the library staff at the Library of Congress, the National Archives, the Nuclear Regulatory Commission and the Federal Bureau of Investigation. Thank you all.

TABLE OF CONTENTS

CHAPTER ONE

DEFINING THE THREAT

"We are at war against infidels. Take this
message with you - I ask all Islamic nations,
all Muslims, all Islamic armies and all
heads of Islamic states to join the holy war.
There are many enemies to be killed or
destroyed. Jihad must triumph."
-Iranian leader Ayatollah Khomeini.
-January 14, 1980[1].

"The U.S. is the devil on this planet."
-World Islamic Popular Command.
-March, 1990[2].

I. Prologue: The Cold War Legacy

In the next several years, the United States and other Western nations will
face one of the greatest challenges in the history of mankind - How to
effectively counter and protect their citizens against the rise of a hostile,
deadly and rabidly anti-Western form of fundamentalist Islam. Given the
euphoria in the last several years over the end of the Cold War, it is an
open question whether the West will recognize this challenge let alone
meet it. The end of the Cold War has led to many potentially dangerous
and unrealistic expectations. In the field of defense policy, the collapse of
Communism has caused the West, particularly the United States, to
embark upon one of the largest programs of military disarmament in the
history of the world. The arms race has been replaced by a massive and
unprecedented disarmament race, and America has the somewhat dubious
distinction of being in the lead. In our universities, well known academics
have extolled the end of history as we know it. For example, University
of Chicago Professor Francis Fukuyama espoused this view in *The End of
History and the Last Man*[3]. According to Fukuyama and others, democratic ideals supposedly now reign supreme throughout the world, China

and much of the Muslim world notwithstanding. The worldwide competition and clash between cultures and divergent political ideals is alleged to be over for all time. A new era of peace and largely economic competition lies in front of us, say some academics. In a manner of speaking, these commentators believe that conflicts between nations, hemispheres and continents will largely take place in the economic arena and every four years at the Olympics. As this work hopes to make clear, nothing could be further from the truth. Americans and Europeans clearly believe that the world is a safer place since the collapse of Communism in 1989 and 1990. But is it? The bipolar world that existed from 1945 to 1990 clearly presented its own challenges and hazards but it did keep the lid on scores of ethnic and religious hatreds that have now boiled over into armed conflict. With the lid off the Soviet jack in the box, we have seen murderous fighting between Orthodox Christian Armenians and Muslim Azerbaijanis, Orthodox Christian Serbs and Muslim Bosnians, Georgians and the Russian Army, Muslim Chechens and the Russian Army, Tadhziks and their neighbors, etc. Nationalist and religious political movements with ominously racist overtones have also appeared among the White Russians, the Germans (including a resurgent fascism by the skin heads and certain far right parties which seek to glorify Nazism) and the Poles (anti-Semitism reared its ugly head during Poland's national presidential elections). The fervent desire to unite with other peoples of the same ethnic and religious identity, without the concomitant desire for long term peaceful co-existence with other, unrelated groups, has raised the violence quotient of the world immeasurably during the last several years.

One of the stabilizing facts of the Cold War competition was that both East and West kept their client states in check[4]. While some rivalries were fueled during the Cold War others clearly were suppressed by it. The Western and Communist spheres of influence imposed a kind of stable, albeit often ruthless, political symmetry upon the rest of the world. If not a Pax Americana, at least a truce of sorts existed between the two superpowers with fights erupting only at the obscure fringes of the political map. Korea, Vietnam and Afghanistan were political backwaters before the Cold War thrust them into the spotlight.

The Communist ideal gave people of radically different backgrounds and ethnic and religious heritages a common purpose and singular world view which served to unify them. With Communism's collapse, many nations forged in the crucible of Communism have died with it. The peoples of the former Soviet Union and Yugoslavia, for example, have found that there is no longer anything that commonly defines and therefore unites them. Nations have disappeared from the map with astonishing swiftness.

The political universe, like the physical one, abhors a vacuum. Therefore, it is highly likely that new nations as yet unborn and presently only guessed at will spring into being during the final years of the 20th century. The remaining years of this century will be a time of tremendous international change. These changes may not always bode well for the West, particularly if the Islamic peoples of the former Soviet Empire find common cause with the radical, violently anti-Western Islamic regime in Iran to their south.

II. 1980: The Death of One Empire and the Birth of Another

Those now hastily attempting to write the history of the late 20th century trace "the beginning of the end" for the Communist world and the vast changes in the international political landscape that are still unfolding to the largely peaceful revolutions in Eastern Europe that took place in 1989-90. However, in generations to come, 1980 may very well be looked upon as a more pivotal year in world history. Like a number of historically significant years, many of those living at the time (including the author) had little, if any, idea that 1980 would be one of those fulcrums of history which signal the death of the past and the birth of a new and dangerous future.

The rise of the Solidarity trade union movement in Poland during 1980 sounded the death knell for world Communism. The success of Lech Walesa and Solidarity in toppling Poland's communist government would send shock waves throughout the rest of the Iron Curtain in Eastern Europe and would lead to the Velvet Revolution in Czechoslovakia and the bloody revolution in Romania nearly ten years later as people under Communist rule everywhere took heart and saw that the Bolshevik yoke could indeed be thrown off.

Mikhail Gorbachev's attempt to revitalize the Soviet Empire in the face of these challenges was doomed from the start[5]. The gap between Communism's utopian promises and the reality of Communist rule was too great. Furthermore, the example and influence exerted by Western culture, wealth and ideas over the peoples of Eastern Europe and the Soviet Union, particularly the younger generation, was too strong. After nearly 75 years, the Communist revolution had run out of steam and ossified.

While the Soviet Empire was breaking up and dying worldwide, another empire founded on another set of ideals was just being born. The Islamic revolution which had begun in Iran in 1979 was in full fury by 1980[6]. Shah Reza Pahlevi, the leader of Iran, had been forced from power and into exile. Ayatollah Khomeini, an aged Muslim cleric with a fanatical hatred of the West and a rigid, essentially medieval conception of the world, triumphantly entered the capitol city of Tehran and was installed as the absolutist leader of a new, "Islamic Republic of Iran." Interestingly, the Soviet Union's dirty war in Afghanistan, a war it ultimately lost, served both to foreshadow the Soviet Union's own demise as well as showcase the newest actors on the world stage - the fundamentalist Muslims who served in the Afghan resistance.

The new Islamic regime in Iran was clearly hostile to the West, as many American, Canadian and European businessmen, diplomats and their families living in that nation were soon to discover[7]. American businessmen were imprisoned and American diplomats were taken hostage and repeatedly paraded before the media bound and wearing blindfolds, an infamous and degrading spectacle that came to be known popularly as the Iranian hostage crisis. Iranian citizens themselves also suffered at the hands of this religious regime. Many became the victims of mass executions and imprisonment that continued for months and years as the Ayatollah Khomeini and his followers murdered or imprisoned anyone they suspected might not be sympathetic to their brand of fundamentalist Islam. The successful entrepreneurial and commercial classes, members of government and mid-level to senior officers in the Iranian military suffered particularly egregiously[8]. These unfortunates were persecuted and killed either because of their ties to the prior regime or because, particularly in the case of wealthy Iranians, they were accused of being "too Western" in outlook, manners and dress. The Muslim leadership would later come to regret during Iran's ghastly eight year war with Iraq its mass execution of senior Iranian military officers during the early days of the Iranian Revolution[9]. The slaughter or imprisonment of wealthy Iranians has also hurt Iran's more recent attempts to revitalize its economy.

The revolution in Iran gave the modern world its first, hard look at a fundamentalist Islamic dictatorship in power, and the picture was a bloody one.   Relations with such a nation were virtually impossible since the Islamic Republic of Iran abrogated many of its treaty obligations, sneered at international law and openly derided such ancient rules between nations as the sanctity of diplomatic embassies and staff.   As a matter of state policy, the revolutionary government was also stridently anti-Western and vehemently opposed to all non-Islamic cultural, religious, artistic and intellectual influences.

Since the early days of the Islamic revolution inside Iran, the threat of fundamentalist Islam to world peace and human progress and advancement has only grown larger.   Islamic fundamentalism, by its own words and deeds, is openly hostile to Western society and institutions.   The World Trade Center bombing in New York City on February 26, 1993 which killed 6 people and injured 1,000 and the foiled plan by Islamic radicals to assassinate United States Senator Alphonse D'Amato, United Nations Secretary General Boutros Ghali and Egyptian President Mubarak as well as to bomb two heavily used New York City tunnels are only the most recent examples of the danger posed by this worldwide revolutionary movement[10].   Iran's death sentence[11] against British author Salman Rushdie which Iran announced on February 14, 1989 for a work of fiction Mr. Rushdie wrote entitled *The Satanic Verses*[12] demonstrates the profound chasm between Western society, which practices tolerance and encourages the free exchange of ideas, and this violent and intolerant breed of Islam which persecutes and kills dissenters and free thinkers wherever and whenever it finds them.

Islamic fundamentalist forces are hard at work and may soon seize power in Egypt (under the Muslim Brotherhood or related radical Islamic groups), Algeria (under the banner of the Islamic Salvation Front), Morocco, Tunisia and the Central Asian republics of the former Soviet Union which boast a largely Muslim population, to name only a few countries.   While Muslim activists in these countries publicly claim that their efforts are aimed at peaceful conquest through the ballot box, terrorism against innocent Western tourists and citizens including the shooting of tourists at popular historic sites in Egypt is plainly also part of their cold blooded takeover strategy.   Looking at deeds and not just words, it is clear that many Islamic activists have learned to manipulate the media and public opinion in the West and in their own countries by speaking the language of democracy, while secretly practising terrorism as a way of undermining legitimate regimes.

In the final years of this century and the beginning of the next, Islamic fundamentalist forces will most likely rise to power in many countries throughout North Africa, the Middle East and Asia and will spread as far as the Indian subcontinent and Indonesia. Like Iran and Sudan, the two linchpins of the modern Islamic revolution, these new governments will be openly hostile to Western governments, institutions, culture and ideas. Given the West's experiences with the Islamic Republic of Iran, relations with these nations will be tenuous at best and may very well be actively hostile. The chances of military conflict between a future "Islamic bloc" and the current Western bloc countries will be high.

III. Nukes on the Loose and Other Dangers

Bloody conflict between the Judeo-Christian and Muslim worlds has occurred many times before over the centuries. Western armies have clashed with the Moors in Spain, have fought throughout the Mediterranean and Middle East during the Crusades and have twice battled Muslim armies outside the gates of Vienna in an effort to stop the Muslims from sacking Central Europe[14]. The venerable Byzantine Empire lost its centuries-long battle with Islam when Suleyeiman the Magnificent of the Ottoman Empire besieged and sacked Constantinople in May of 1453[15]. The Ottoman Turks burned and pillaged the capitol city and raped and slaughtered many of its inhabitants for a period of three days after the Byzantines' surrender. Scores of ancient and irreplaceable books, artifacts, manuscripts and works of art were utterly destroyed in the process and lost to humanity for all time. More recently, Israeli armies have fought modern day Muslims in several regional wars including the 1967 Six Day War and the 1973 Yom Kippur War[16].

The fundamentalist Muslims clearly have grandiose dreams of world power and, according to their own public statements, murderous intentions toward Western citizens and their respective governments. What makes fanatical Muslims dangerous however, is not just the size of the countries they control or their sheer numbers but the ease with which they are now able to obtain nuclear, chemical and biological weapons of mass destruction. With the collapse of the Soviet Union and the loss of effective control over large parts of the vast Soviet military and nuclear arsenal, it has never been easier for terrorists and Third World dictators to get their hands on nuclear weapons. In order to raise cash or barter for needed goods, some of the former Soviet republics have actually been willing to entertain offers for their military hardware. The largest weapons bazaar in world history continues apace throughout Eastern Europe and Asia after the collapse of Soviet communism.

The security danger looming over the West like some vast yet unseen cloud has two components - the growing military danger posed by fundamentalist Muslim nations like Iran and Sudan and the danger posed by fundamentalist Muslim terrorists and other groups who are now able to obtain nuclear devices and other weapons of mass destruction. Each of these threats is discussed in turn[17].

The religious dictatorship headquartered in Tehran has been steadily building the size and strength of its military forces through black market and other purchases of sophisticated Soviet weaponry and military technology. In addition to increasing the size of its conventional military since the end of the Iran-Iraq War in 1988, the Islamic Republic of Iran has gone to great lengths to recruit impoverished Soviet scientists and to buy advanced missiles (capable of carrying nuclear, biological or chemical devices) from China, North Korea and from the international black market[18].

To cite only a few examples out of many, the Islamic Republic of Iran has quietly purchased several Kirov-class Soviet submarines and has bought large quantities of Sukhoi-24s, MiG-29s, Su-22s, tanks, artillery pieces and armored personnel carriers[19]. Iran also continues to buy sophisticated missiles, chemical weaponry and other advanced military technology from China and North Korea[20]. With the assistance of China, North Korea and Pakistan, Iran is moving rapidly toward becoming a nuclear power[21]. It has been reported that the CIA believes Iran already has successfully recruited Russian nuclear scientists and engineers[22]. The Islamic Republic of Iran's effort to develop its own home-grown nuclear bomb is centered at Moallem Kelaieh, that nation's supersecret nuclear weapons complex located northwest of Tehran[23]. In April, 1992 the respected journal *The European* reported that Iran had covertly purchased nuclear weapons from parties inside the former Soviet Union[24]. Another published source concludes that Iran has purchased at least three tactical nuclear missiles from Kazakhstan[25]. Thus, Iran may already be a member of the nuclear club, despite the West's most earnest wishes for a non-nuclear Middle East.

No one should doubt Iran's will and ability to use nuclear weapons where it deems necessary. During the Iran-Iraq War, Iran kidnapped its own schoolchildren from playgrounds and soccer fields and forced them to run on the battlefield in "human waves" in order to clear minefields and draw machine gun fire away from its regular soldiers. Such a regime, its protestations of religious intolerance and bigotry notwithstanding, has shown itself to be capable of committing acts of great evil worthy of a Stalin or Hitler.

Another aspect of the military danger faced by the West has to do with the ease with which nuclear and other weapons may now be purchased or smuggled from the territory of the former Soviet Union. While countries like Iran, North Korea and others have capitalized on the bargains available, this situation has really been of most benefit to non-governmental entities like the Russian mafia and various terrorist groups looking to increase their visibility and "clout." The Congressional Office of Technology Assessment has researched the problem of proliferation and has concluded, in part, that the political authorities in each of the former republics do not necessarily control what goes on inside each of their territories[26]. In the absence of centralized Soviet military control, nuclear, chemical and biological weapons and weapon material (such as plutonium and uranium) located within the former Soviet Union have become increasingly difficult to track and some have simply "disappeared."[27] In fact, there has never been an accurate accounting by the Russians, the other former Soviet republics or anyone else of the precise amount of nuclear material in existence inside the former Soviet Union[28]. Proposals to identify, locate and "tag" all such nuclear material have met with resistance from a number of quarters. For example, the Natural Resources Defense Council's suggestion that former Soviet scientists work with a U.S. team to identify and track the whereabouts of all nuclear weapons and material has not yet been implemented largely because of a Russian demand (unacceptable to the U.S. Government) that the U.S. also open its own nuclear arsenal to a similar inspection[29]. The NRDC's proposal had the advantage of employing impoverished personnel in the former Soviet Union at a time when they are facing increasingly enticing demands to practice their nuclear craft abroad[30].

The former Soviet Union is a veritable smuggler's paradise. The Western press, particularly in Germany, has published numerous accounts of attempted smuggling incidents involving nuclear material[31]. The Russian mafia has apparently gotten into the act, running stolen or illegally purchased nuclear and military technology through its drug transportation channels[32]. Louis J. Freeh, currently the director of the F.B.I., told the United States Senate Government Affairs Committee in May, 1994 that the Russian mafia has been attempting to obtain and smuggle atomic material out of Russia for sale on the international black market[33]. Mr. Freeh stated that the F.B.I. was "gravely concerned [that] Russian organized crime members may have already attained or will attain the capacity to steal nuclear weapons."[34] Mr. Freeh's concerns were echoed by Mikhail Yegorov, head of the organized crime control department of the Russian Ministry of Internal Affairs[35]. Mr. Yegorov stated before the same Congressional committee that "[t]hese crime groups in recent years are demonstrating more and more interest toward the defense facilities of the former Soviet Union."[36]

The exponential growth of Russian organized crime and the nuclear threat that such illicit organizations pose to the world community have been the subject of at least two government reports. The Department of Energy's Z Division located at the Lawrence Livermore Laboratory in Livermore, California, studies nuclear proliferation issues. The Z Division has access to the most highly classified intelligence on the existence and spread of nuclear weapons and technology. Uneasy over the growing role of organized crime in the spread of nuclear weapons, the U.S. Government has directed the Z Division to extensively analyze the nuclear threat posed by the Russian mafia[37]. Similarly, the Department of Energy's Office of Threat Assessment has also reported on the role of organized crime inside the former Soviet Union in the spread of nuclear weapons and military technology worldwide[38]. The OTA concluded in its report that one quarter of Russian organized crime groups have ties to criminal organizations outside the former Soviet republics[39].

Corruption in the army and elements of the police and civil service is also widespread[40]. Military facilities are inadequately guarded by demoralized, poorly armed and poorly paid soldiers who are vulnerable to bribes and other inducements to smuggle arms and other weapons[41]. In February of 1993 alone, stated the OTA report, the Russian military announced that it planned to discipline 3,000 officers for questionable business practices and to court-martial 46 general officers on corruption and bribery charges[42].

These government studies and reports indicate that the U.S. Government is clearly concerned about the role of organized crime in the theft and proliferation of nuclear weapons and material. At the same time, U.S. officials don't want to panic American citizens. Consequently, the deteriorating situation inside Russia and the other former Soviet republics and the exponential growth of the Russian mafia has been publicly minimized. As one American official who wished to remain anonymous put it: "I'm a very strong supporter of freedom of the press...But even an investigative reporter would support the notion that you don't yell 'Fire' in a theater."[43] A former national security advisor during both the Reagan and Bush Administrations compared the situation in Russia and the former Soviet republics to 1930s Chicago "except that Al Capone has access to nuclear weapons."[44] American diplomatic and military personnel have also feared damaging or ending their careers if they spoke out publicly on the record about these alarming developments[45].

By all indications, former Soviet installations containing nuclear weapons are old, broken down and poorly guarded. The weapons most at risk are tactical nuclear warheads[46]. However, even the plutonium used in civilian nuclear reactors is a target for theft because of its value in making literally hundreds of nuclear bombs. As U.S. and Russian officials have privately admitted, the actual on-base security systems presently in place for protecting nuclear fuel or weapons components are appallingly inadequate. Locks easily can be picked or blown off, assuming they even exist. In fact at one nuclear storage site in Russia enriched uranium was stored in a Quonset hut with only a padlock for protection[47]. The soldiers detailed to guard the site were armed with hunting knives[48].

Security in the Soviet Union was founded upon the principle of rigid centralized control and tight border security[49]. Under the old Soviet system, military and nuclear security always worked because the entire country was run like a prison, with two divisions of KGB personnel and a rigorously trained and professional border patrol ready to track down anyone who attempted to smuggle a nuclear device out of the country.

Thieves might be able to overwhelm a crew at a given storage site or missile silo but they would never get out of the country alive.

But the new Russia no longer has the money or the stomach to bring back the old KGB. Military and civilian nuclear installations have few if any security systems in place. Personnel are poorly paid and can't be trusted[50]. Scientists at some facilities are more worried about housing and health care than they are about keeping nuclear secrets and devices out of the hands of unscrupulous foreign governments[51]. Guards are willing to sell their precious nuclear charges for the right price as is evident from several recent incidents.

In 1991 a former U.S. Army intelligence officer named William M. Arkin attempted to demonstrate the ease with which nuclear weapons could be illicitly purchased from the Russians. He engaged in secret negotiations with a Russian lieutenant for the purchase of a nuclear missile[52]. The missile was a nuclear tipped SCUD weighing 1,500 pounds[53]. The Russian lieutenant was stationed at Alten-Grabow, a Soviet military base outside of Berlin[54]. For approximately $250,000, the lieutenant agreed to load the missile at night onto a flatbed truck and drive it off the base[55].

Security at the base consisted of a mere 12 soldiers, all of whom reported to the corrupt lieutenant and at least 2 of whom were apparently willing to help Arkin and the lieutenant smuggle the nuclear missile out of its silo and off the military base[56]. The plan was unexpectedly interrupted by the August, 1991 coup attempt in Moscow at which time all nuclear weapons and associated military personnel were abruptly ordered out of Germany[57].

This true story is matched by another one reported by a Russian journalist named Kirill Belyaninov, a reporter for the respected Russian newsmagazine *Literaturnaya Gazeta*[58]. Belyaninov went underground to establish contact with the nuclear black market inside Russia[59]. He was soon offered a Soviet SS-20 nuclear missile for $70,000[60]. The reporter was offered a photo of the merchandise prior to purchase[61]. He took the photo to scientists at Arzamas-16, a Russian nuclear weapons laboratory[62]. The Russian scientists concluded that the warhead appeared authentic[63]. The weapon was never purchased because *Literaturnaya Gazeta* did not have $70,000 with which to consummate the deal[64].

Both incidents provide hard evidence that nuclear weapons are easily obtainable for a price. Paul A. Goble, a former State Department official and special advisor on Soviet nationality issues now with the Carnegie Endowment for International Peace, recently stated: "I'm convinced that if I had twenty-five million dollars, I could buy a warhead and the launch codes." As the above incidents demonstrate, some nuclear weapons are even available for a lot less than that[65].

What hasn't been smuggled out is apparently for sale by the former Soviet republics themselves. There is real suspicion within Western military and intelligence circles that poorer republics have been willing to sell their advanced military technology, including longe range missiles and chemical and nuclear weapons, for hard cash[66]. Impoverished military personnel, weapons experts and nuclear technicians from the former Soviet Union are also currently available to the highest interested bidder. So far, the most avid bidders have been the newly emergent Islamic regimes or other outlaw Third World nations such as Libya and Syria which regularly make the U.S. State Department list of terrorist countries. In fact, it has been reported that Iran has successfully recruited nuclear scientists for its military program[67].

Estimating conservatively, there are at least 30,000 nuclear warheads (many still pre-targeted at North American and Western European cities and military-industrial installations) in the former Soviet Union's military arsenal. Until recently, the CIA believed that the former Soviet Union had about 35,000 nuclear warheads[68]. However, Russian atomic energy minister Mikhailov revealed that the old Soviet Union actually had 45,000 nuclear warheads[69]. The West has similarly underestimated the amount of highly enriched uranium the former Soviet republics possess. The U.S. thought Russia had 500 tons[70]. Mikhailov recently stated the amount was almost three times that figure[71]. The largely Muslim nation of Kazakhstan alone still has 104 SS-18 missiles and 40 nuclear armed bombers on its soil which it has been reluctant to give up or destroy[72]. It is quite possible that a number of these doomsday machines may fall into the hands of radical Islamic regimes openly hostile to the West.

Recent revelations from Russia about the existence of a Soviet "Doomsday Device" designed to survive a massive U.S. nuclear first strike and launch a counterstrike automatically without human intervention are also troubling[73]. This device poses a threat to the West because elements of the Doomsday Device may be seized and/or exploited by Islamic radicals or the Russian mafia with the intention of blackmailing or launching an unprovoked nuclear strike against the United States or Europe. The Soviet Doomsday Device is also an ongoing threat to Western citizens because the lack of proper maintenance over time may cause the device to degrade and accidentally trigger a massive nuclear launch.

The following three chapters will explain in more detail the history and sources of Islamic hatred of the West, past attempts to unite the Muslim Middle East and why at the end of the present century such efforts at unification may very well succeed. In 'The Threat At Home,' the author will discuss America's vulnerability to terrorist acts on its own soil and our nation's inability to deal effectively with the threat of domestic terrorism at the present time. Finally, a plan of action will be set forth containing several concrete recommendations for dealing effectively with both the threat at home and the threat abroad.

§ § §

ENDNOTES

1.   Laffin, *Holy War: Islam Fights*, 13-14.

2.   JANA, March 20, 1990.

3.   Fukuyama, *The End of History and the Last Man*.

4.   For a general history of the Cold War, see LaFeber, *America, Russia, and the Cold War: 1945-1980*. For a probing and insightful analysis of relations between the U.S. and U.S.S.R. see Ulam, *The Rivals: America and Russia Since World War II*.

5.   See generally Beschloss and Talbott, *At The Highest Levels: The Inside Story Of The End Of The Cold War*.

6.   For a history of modern Iran and the early years of the Iranian Revolution, see Keddie, *Roots of Revolution: An Interpretive History of Modern Iran*. See also, *IRAN'S REVOLUTION   The Search for Consensus*, R.K. Ramazani, ed.; Wright, *SACRED RAGE: The Wrath of Militant Islam*, 26-45; Hunter, *IRAN AND THE WORLD: Continuity in a Revolutionary Decade*.

7.   For a true account of the trials and tribulations of a group of American businessmen stranded in Iran during the early days of the Iranian Revolution, see Follett, *On Wings of Eagles*.

8.   Phillips, "The Saddamization of Iran," 6, 9.

9.   Ibid.

10.   "The New Terrorism," *Newsweek*, 23 (July 5, 1993).

11.   *The Rushdie Letters: Freedom to Speak, Freedom to Write*, 9.

12.   Salman Rushdie's *The Satanic Verses* was first published by Viking in 1989.

13.   Miller, "The Challenge of Radical Islam," 43.

14.   Huntington, "The Clash of Civilizations," 22, 31.

15.   See generally Vasiliev, *History of the Byzantine Empire*.

16.   Safran, *Israel: The Embattled Ally*, 240-256, 278-316.

17.   For a trenchant analysis of the problem of worldwide nuclear proliferation and what the United States should do about it, see Mandelbaum, "Lessons of the Next Nuclear War," 22-37.

18.   Phillips, "Saddamization of Iran," 6, 9-10; Sick, "Iran: The Adolescent Revolution," 160-163.

19.   Pipes & Clawson, "Ambitious Iran, Troubled Neighbors," 124, 127.

20.   Phillips, "Saddamization of Iran," 9-10.

21.   Ibid; Pipes & Clawson, "Ambitious Iran, Troubled Neighbors," 127.

22.   Hersh, "The Wild East," 61, 76.

23.   Anderson, "Headlines You Could See In 1994," 6.

24.   "Iran Has A-Bomb," *The European*, (April 30, 1992).

25.   Davidson & Rees-Mogg, *The Great Reckoning: Protect Yourself in the Coming Depression*, 223; Olcott, "Central Asia's Catapult to Independence," 108, 119.

26.   Hersh, "The Wild East," 76.

27.   Hersh, "The Wild East," 68-70; "Russian Aide Says Gangsters Try to Steal Atom Material," *The New York Times*, A5 (Thursday, May 26, 1994); "The plutonium racket," *The Economist*, 39-40 (August 20-26, 1994); "Empty Containers," *U.S. News & World Report*, 22 (April 16, 1992).

28.   Hersh, "The Wild East," 68-69.

29.   Ibid.

30.   Ibid.

31.   See e.g., "The plutonium racket," *The Economist*, 39-40 (August 20-26, 1994); "Uranium, Plutonium, Who's Got the Goods? Nuclear Nations Ask," *Wall Street Journal*, A1, A8 (Wednesday, May 11, 1994); Hersh, "The Wild East," 68, 75.

32.   Hersh, "The Wild East," 75; "Russian Aide Says Gangsters Try to Steal Atom Material," *The New York Times*, A5 (Thursday, May 26, 1994).

33.   "Russian Aide Says Gangsters Try to Steal Atom Material," *The New York Times*, A5 (Thursday, May 26, 1994).

34.   Ibid.

35. Ibid.

36. Ibid.

37. Hersh, "The Wild East," 74-75.

38. Hersh, "The Wild East," 66-68.

39. Ibid.

40. Ibid.

41. Ibid; see generally Hersh, "The Wild East," 66-86.

42. Hersh, "The Wild East," 66-68.

43. Hersh, "The Wild East," 69.

44. Hersh, "The Wild East," 79.

45. Ibid.

46. Hersh, "The Wild East," 68.

47. Hersh, "The Wild East," 76.

48. Ibid.

49. Hersh, "The Wild East," 69.

50. See generally Hersh, "The Wild East," 66-86.

51. Hersh, "The Wild East," 76.

52. Hersh, "The Wild East," 72-74.

53. Hersh, "The Wild East," 72.

54. Ibid.

55. Ibid.

56. Ibid.

57. Ibid.

58. Hersh, "The Wild East," 74.

59. Ibid.

60. Ibid.

61. Ibid.

62. Ibid.

63. Ibid.

64. Ibid.

65. Hersh, "The Wild East," 72.

66. Olcott, "Central Asia's Catapult to Independence," 108, 118-119.

67. Hersh, "The Wild East," 76; Phillips, "Saddamization of Iran," 10.

68. "Uranium, Plutonium, Who's Got the Goods? Nuclear Nations Ask," *Wall Street Journal*, A1, A8 (Wednesday, May 11, 1994).

69. Ibid.

70. Ibid.

71. Ibid.

72. Pipes & Clawson, "Ambitious Iran, Troubled Neighbors," 124, 138.

73.   The existence of the Soviet "Doomsday Device" was widely reported in the autumn of 1993 by most major newspapers and television media. See e.g., *The New York Times*, A6 (October 8, 1993).

CHAPTER TWO

THE THREAT FROM ABROAD

"Death to America, the Great Satan!"
-militant Islamic slogan[1].

"Muslims must kill the enemies of Allah, in
every way and everywhere in order to
liberate themselves from the grandchildren
of the pigs and apes who are educated at the
table of the Zionists, the communists and the
imperialists."
-Sheik Omar Abdel-Rahman.
1992 speech[2].

"Any doubt about the need to struggle
against the U.S. means being enslaved by
the Great Satan and losing the honor and
the life the Islamic Revolution has brought
to this country and the whole Islamic
Ummah (community of believers)."
-Ali Akbar Mohtashemi, Iranian government
official.
-July 18, 1990[3].

Islam is the fastest growing religion in the world. It is also one of the
largest organized religions in existence with a worldwide membership
conservatively estimated to be at least 850 million or over one sixth of all
humanity[4]. Muslims as a group constitute the majority or near majority
of people living in North Africa, the Middle East, Southern and Central
Asia, the Balkans and Indonesia[5]. When in control of government,
Muslims have set the tone and defined the parameters of acceptable
political and intellectual discourse. Out of power, they have formed a
brooding, restive and sometimes volatile population which is often feared
and distrusted by those in government. Communists in both the former
Soviet Union and China have worked systematically to suppress Islamic

cultural and religious folkways among their Muslim or Muslim-leaning citizens. Indeed, in the 1920s and 1930s Stalin created the boundaries of the Soviet Central Asian Republics with the aim of splitting indigenous ethnic groups and breaking the power of Islam in the region[6]. This goal was further advanced by the forced resettlement of some of the native peoples who were shipped from Central Asia to Siberia and the state planned importation of ethnic Russians to live in the area[7]. So what is Islam and why is it such a potent force in national and regional politics?

I. History and Origins of Islam

Islam originated as a religion in the early 600s AD[8]. At that time, a young Arab named Mohammed began to preach the word of God to the citizens of Mecca, a town located on the Arabian peninsula. Mohammed's teachings were based on divine revelation and instructions that Mohammed received from God during his walks in the desert. Unlike Jesus Christ who is portrayed in Christianity as Himself divine, Islam does not portray Mohammed as God but as the mere human messenger of God.

Mohammed's preaching was not well received at first by the citizens of Mecca, primarily because Mohammed's injunctions were viewed as an attack upon the pretensions and way of life of the rich merchants and traders who dominated the city and who had little interest in religion generally. After threats were made against his personal safety, Mohammed moved to the settlement of Medina in 622 AD which is located 200 miles to the north of Mecca. The date of this migration or *hijra* would later mark the starting point of the Muslim calendar. In Medina, Mohammed was able to establish a solid base of operations and a core group of followers without outside interference. It is important for us today as we confront the political face of radical Islam to understand that Mohammed exercised not only spiritual leadership but also political leadership in Medina, thus cementing Islam's dual character as a religion which offers both spiritual principles and guidance and a concrete and immutable set of rules governing the structure and organization of society.

From his time in Medina onward, Mohammed followed the traditional path of a revolutionary leader, exercising both political and military leadership on behalf of the community of believers or *umma*. Trading caravans from Mecca were periodically attacked and the town itself was later occupied by Mohammed's fledgling band of followers in 630 AD.

Mohammed's exercise of political as well as religious power was to have a lasting impact on Islam throughout the centuries. Each of Mohammed's successors acted not only as the *imam* or spiritual leader for the community but also as the commander of the faithful or *caliph*. Thus, political and religious power are traditionally one and the same. In the "Islamic Republic" of Iran today, for example, the *ulama* or Islamic scholars occupy high government positions, and the polity itself is founded upon and operated based on traditional Islamic principles. Having experienced persecution early in its history, the Muslim religion adopted from the very start a hardy and war-like posture vis-a-vis non-Muslim groups. Warfare was expected and regularly occurred between adherents of the new religion and others in the region. Part and parcel of the new religion was the concept of *jihad* or holy war against non-Muslims. Mohammed and his successors carried on a *jihad* for many years until all other political regimes in a wide geographic area surrounding the "cradle of Islam" on the Arabian peninsula had succumbed to Muslim rule. By the 8th century, Islam under the great Arab empire which gave the religion its political face had spread as far as northern Spain in the West and deep into Asia and India to the East[9]. The Battle of Tours in 732 AD marked political Islam's furthest reach up the Iberian peninsula into France[10].

II. Islam's "Golden Age"

Upon Mohammed's death in 632 AD one of his followers named Abu Bakr ruled as *caliph* (which also means successor to the Messenger of God)[11]. Abu Bakr was the founder of the Ummayyad dynasty which lasted from 661-750 AD[12]. From 750 until the fall of Baghad to the Mongols in 1258, the Abbasids ruled what historians today call the Arab empire[13]. The Muslims generally led the world during these years in science, medicine, astronomy, warfare, engineering, art, architecture, town planning, sanitation, education and several other fields[14]. In fact, it is through the Muslim world and the Arab empire in particular that much of our knowledge of the ancient classical world derives. Classical authors survived in translation in Arab libraries during Europe's Dark Ages after which time they were re-introduced to the people of Europe via Arabia.

As the Arab empire withered during the Middle Ages, the Ottoman Empire took shape and began to expand outward from the region of modern Turkey known in ancient times as Anatolia. This regime too was based on the common culture and belief system afforded by Islam. In material and intellectual terms, the Ottoman Empire led to another "Golden Age" for Islam[15]. At their height, the Ottomans controlled a greater land mass than the Romans had[16].

By the 16th century, the Ottoman Turks controlled the Black Sea and Crimea to the north, Greece, Bosnia, Serbia, Romania and Hungary (after the Battle of Mohacs in 1526) in eastern Europe and all of the Middle East and Egypt stretching to North Africa and Spain in the West[17]. The Ottomans struck fear into the hearts of the Europeans during their repeated assaults on Vienna in the 1500s and again as late as 1683. These assaults were ultimately unsuccessful and marked the high water mark of Islamic territorial gains in Central Europe.

From the 16th century onwards, the Ottoman Empire slowly sank into military, moral and political weakness and decay[18]. The Western powers leapt ahead in military technology, science and learning and pushed the Ottomans back upon their ancestral lands in Turkey[19]. By the 19th century, the Ottoman Empire was derisively known as the "Sick Man of Europe," a nation that was constantly being propped up or dismembered, as the situation warranted, by the European monarchies[20]. Ottoman rule was finally extinguished at the end of World War I[21]. It is this earlier period that Muslims look back upon with pride even as they often look upon their present situation with feelings of humiliation, anger and shame.

During the height of the Arab and Ottoman Empires, Muslim culture and learning flourished. Great universities such as Al-Azhar University in Cairo were founded during these years. During this time period, Islam was an extraordinarily vibrant and compelling religion with a crusading spirit and a zeal for territorial expansion.

In addition to these two great empires, other Islamic regimes have flourished including the Moghul Empire which was based in the vicinity of modern Afghanistan and Pakistan and which eventually won through military conquest the rest of the Indian subcontinent[22]. The Safavid dynasty, representing the Shi'a branch of Islam, ruled in Persia[23]. Individuals living as far east as Indonesia became Muslims through conversion, forcible or otherwise[24].

III. Divisions of Islam, Aspects of the Religion

The Word of God as communicated to Mohammed was eventually embodied in written form in the Koran[25]. Arabic is the language of the Koran and the "mother tongue" of all Muslims. Portions of the Koran incorporate parts of the Bible. The revelations embodied in the Koran are supplemented and more readily understood by reference to the *hadith* or Tradition, meaning what Mohammed himself said or did while alive. The revelations imparted to Mohammed and embodied in the Koran are considered final and apply to all of humanity for all time. Thus, Mohammed has no successor in Islam in the sense of one who would continue to receive divine revelations. Rather, the *imam* , the Muslim community's individual spiritual leader, or the learned men of Islam known as the *ulama*, can only study what God has already said in the Koran and interpret its contents for the masses.

Islamic law, known as the *sharia*, governs virtually all aspects of an individual believer's life[26]. In contrast to Western politics and theology, there is no division in Islam between the secular and religious spheres of life and certainly no distinction between politics and government on the one hand and religious life and institutions on the other[27]. Religion pervades all politics. All political positions are founded on or interpreted according to religious tenets. Since the "state" in a Western sense is founded on the Koran, dissent is not just a political act it is a sin against God![28] The principle that there is no separation between religion and politics is a central tenet of the present day Islamic fundamentalists. In a speech to his students at Najaf years before rising to power in Iran, Khomeini angrily declared:

> The slogan of the separation of religion and politics and the
> demand that Islamic scholars should not intervene in social or
> political affairs have been formulated and propagated by the

imperialists; it is only the irreligious who repeat them. Were
religion and politics separate at the time of the Prophet...?[29]

Marriage, sex, family relationships, commercial and banking activities,
criminal behavior, legal relations and methods of religious observance are
all addressed somewhere in the Koran or the *sharia* which has sprung up
from that holy text. The Koran and its legal tradition regulate virtually
every sphere of an Islamic individual's life. For example, those countries
or communities governed according to Islamic law refer directly to
religious sources in determining how to punish certain crimes. The Koran
prescribes specific punishments for several crimes. Unlawful intercourse
is punished by stoning. False accusation of unlawful intercourse calls for
the application of 100 lashes. Drinking wine will earn the individual 80
lashes. Theft is punished by cutting off a hand or foot. If homicide occurs
during a robbery then the punishment is death. There are several dietary
restrictions as well in addition to the prohibition against imbibing alcohol.
Islamic law also makes its presence felt in the commercial sphere. Usury
and the charging of interest on loans is generally forbidden as is gambling.
The prohibition against charging interest called *riba* springs from chapter
3, verse 130 of the Koran which states: "Believers! Do not live on interest,
doubled and redoubled!"[30] Thus, it is said that Islam provides the *shari'a*
or total way of life ordained by God for humanity.

Islam has splintered into several sects over time[31]. The most significant
division in the Muslim world is the division between Sunni and Shi'a Islam.
Most Muslims (approximately 85%) are Sunnis[32]. Sunni Islam accepts a
wide variety of religious opinion and historically has been more tolerant
of a diversity of religious viewpoints within Islam. The Arab and Ottoman
empires discussed above were Sunni-dominated regimes.

In contrast, Shi'a Islam has historically been the sect of the poor,
downtrodden and oppressed. It has served as the organizing principle for
political outsiders, revolutionaries and those fighting whatever regime has
been in power. Shi'a Islam claims the largest number of followers after
the Sunnis. Shi'ites today live mostly in Iran, the southern part of modern
day Iraq, the eastern shore of the Arabian peninsula and Azerbaijan.

The split between the Sunnis and Shi'ites began in 644 AD when the third
caliph, Uthman of the Ummayya clan, alienated members of the military

and others by engaging in nepotism in making certain political appointments. Uthman also attempted to impose uniformity upon the budding community of believers by issuing an "authorized" version of the Koran and destroying all others. Uthman was killed by a mutinous band of soldiers in 656 and the Prophet's cousin and son-in-law Ali was then heralded by the mutineers as the new *caliph*. Ali's claim to power was challenged by Uthman's relative, Mu'awiya. After the death of both Mu'awiya and Ali, Mu'awiya's son, Yazid fought and eventually defeated Ali's sons Hasan and Husain thus reclaiming political power for the Ummayyid dynasty.

Those supportive of Ali's claim to the *caliphate* were known as *Shi'at Ali*, or the party of Ali. They became the focus of opposition to the ruling Ummayyids and the source of several revolts. In Shi'a Islam, the piety and virtue of Mohammed's family is often contrasted with the wicked worldliness of the powerful Ummayyids. Themes of martyrdom, death and defeat run throughout Shi'a Islam. For example, Husain's death at the Battle of Karbala in 680 AD at the hands of Yazid is a central story for the sect which is commemorated annually in plays and processions.

Shi'a Islam is, quite simply, the religion of the outsider and the underdog within the Muslim world[33]. As such, it has been the weapon revolutionaries have often chosen for garnering support among the young and poor against non-Muslim or superficially Muslim governments in the Middle East and North Africa. Shi'a Islam and its subsidiary branches (which are not discussed here) is the religious sect which the West commonly labels "militant," "radical" or "fundamentalist," although certain Sunni groups have also been radicalized including the regime in Sudan and Sunni opposition groups throughout North Africa.

IV. Hostility Toward the West

There are several sources of the Islamic world's hostility toward the West. The Arab-Israeli conflict placed the United States and much of Western Europe in Israel's camp thus creating tension with the Islamic nations that exist in the region[34]. The Cold War further promoted this trend. As a counterweight to the West's generally pro-Israel stance, the U.S.S.R. threw its support behind the Arab powers during the 1967 Six Day War and again during the 1973 Yom Kippur War. Many Muslims still resent the

West's championing of Israel's cause during these two conflicts. But the roots of the conflict between Islam and the West go much deeper.

Western and Islamic visions of the state, the individual and society are not only divergent, they are often totally at odds. In the realm of political thought, fundamentalist Islam perceives state authority and legitimacy as springing directly from God[35]. In contrast, modern Western political thought asserts that governmental power arises from the governed. The two cultures are diametrically opposed in this regard. Given the West's emphasis and respect for individual rights and liberties, Western political theory has generally carved out a cluster of personal freedoms with which the state cannot interfere. Thus, Western governments typically do not envision a role for themselves in regulating the intellectual, religious, artistic and political beliefs of their citizens. In practical terms this means that the media, the press and the artistic and publishing communities historically have been free from strict government regulation of their actions and content. The only significant limitation on content comes from the free market. If the consuming public does not like a given book, newspaper or TV show, then that item will eventually be extinguished by economic forces in the marketplace of ideas.

In contrast, the Muslim religion does not distinguish between the religious and secular spheres. Islam's prescriptions, injunctions and instructions reach into virtually every corner of an individual's daily life. The entire community of believers is to be governed according to the Koran and *sharia* or Islamic law. As a consequence, the Islamic world finds it hard to accept that Western governments do not enforce a uniform, society-wide moral code that reaches into the most intimate aspects of their citizens' lives.

The free exchange of ideas within Western society inevitably leads to certain forms of expression, artistic and otherwise, which Muslims among others may find objectionable. For example, traditional Muslims would have a hard time understanding how America's state and federal authorities could permit some videos to be shown on MTV or certain works of art such as Robert Mapplethorpe's homoerotic photographs to be displayed in private museums. The Muslim 'man on the street' cannot understand that Western governments, politicians and political institutions do not necessarily 'approve' of the content of such activities or exhibits merely by virtue of allowing them to exist. As a general matter, the Western democracies simply view artistic and intellectual expression as generally falling outside the province of government influence and regulation. But this distinction often gets lost when the Muslim world views the West. As a result, many Muslims perceive Western society, citizens and forms of government as themselves wicked and morally decayed.

The world has become smaller as a result of expanding world trade, the prevalence of a worldwide media and international telecommunications. The growth of international communication networks (e.g., CNN) and the prevalence of Western popular culture (e.g., Western clothing, American and British rock music) throughout the world have pushed in upon the boundaries of Islamic society and have caused strict Islamists to feel increasingly threatened. Satellite television channels such as MTV and syndicated American television shows such as "Dallas" often reach predominantly Islamic audiences and are taken very seriously by the *ulama* as challenges to Islamic culture and morals.

Islamic fundamentalist parties, terrorists and terrorist regimes have viewed Western culture as a threat to Islam that must be ruthlessly attacked and, if at all possible, even exterminated. In a sense, America's "crime" in radical Muslim eyes is simply that America is America, i.e., a free and open society that is tolerant of different viewpoints. L. Paul Bremer, former head of the United States State Department's counter-terrorism office, says that this is something difficult for Americans to understand:

> [T]he agenda of these people [Muslim fundamentalists] is to attack us for what we are...They don't like American culture, our movies, pornography, women, etc. It's something very hard for Americans who live in a multi-cultured and secular society to understand...[36]

Unlike many terror groups, Islamic terrorist demands are generally not territorial. They do not want to liberate particular lands per se. (Israel being the one exception to this statement.) Rather, the radical Muslims find the very existence of Western culture and ideas hateful and repugnant. Accordingly, in a very real sense the West could not accede to fundamentalist Muslim "demands" even if it wanted to because the fundamentalist

Muslims demand nothing less than complete self-annihilation. Short of jumping into a cultural gas chamber, the West can never truly satisfy Islamic fundamentalists. This is why fruitful dialogue with such factions, not to mention regular diplomatic relations, is ultimately impossible.

The Islamic world's hostility also springs from more prosaic roots. As the Muslim world fell behind the West in science, technology, education, military arts and many other fields during the Ottoman decline, Muslims felt increasingly resentful and insecure[37]. They questioned the greatness of their faith. If they were living according to God's law, then why were they falling behind as a civilization?

This attitude manifested itself in many ways. Muslims in Ottoman Turkey started to feel insecure about wearing the fez, a hat which was a standard item of dress for Ottoman men. In fact, the fez was banned for a period of time since it had come to symbolize backwardness to the political leadership[38]. Muslims were also suspicious and resentful of Western science and astronomy. In one instance, a Muslim military detachment destroyed an observatory in 1580 because they believed it was responsible for bringing an outbreak of the plague to a nearby settlement[39].

The Muslim world's hostility and concern over the West's growing military, economic and scientific superiority fed upon itself and only served to exacerbate the situation. Instead of steadily embracing Western advances, Islam was by turns contemptuous of and eager to learn more about Western technology. For example, despite their stunning defeat at the Battle of Lepanto in 1571 by Catholic Spain and several other Christian powers, the Ottoman Turks declined to adopt Western modes of warfare such as larger fighting galleons and lighter cast-iron cannons which would have modernized their fighting force and placed it on par with their Western adversaries[40]. Like Russia under Peter the Great, Islam under the stewardship of the Ottoman Turks would at other times embark upon a "crash course" to modernize Islamic society completely[41]. Western advisors would be called in to make improvements to the army and the navy and to train civilian members of government in the fundamentals of administering an empire[42]. In addition, promising Ottoman youths would be sent to Europe in order to receive a Western education which was viewed as the best and most advanced education then available[43].

Islamic hostility toward the West continues into our own day, as evidenced by the actions and statements of the leaders of Iran, Sudan, Libya and various Islamic terror groups such as Hezbollah, Islamic Jihad and Hamas. Such hostility has manifested itself in numerous acts of terrorism against Western citizens including the downing of a Boeing 747 aircraft over Lockerbie, Scotland in 1988, the bombing of the World Trade Center on February 26, 1993, and the plot to blow up targets in New York City and to assassinate public officials including the head of the United Nations and U.S. Senator Alphonse D'Amato. The assassination scheme appeared to have been orchestrated by a Muslim cleric living in the United States, Sheik Omar Abdel Rahman, and to have been actively yet secretly supported by the Islamic fundamentalist government of Sudan. Sudan's state sponsorship of terrorism recently earned it a place on the U.S. State Department's list of terrorist countries. The taking of Western hostages in the 1980s by fundamentalist groups operating in Lebanon and materially supported by Iran provides still another example of fundamentalist Islam's ongoing war against the West.

Islamic hatred of the West is not limited to terror organizations. The populace at large of these nations also shares many of these feelings of extreme hostility. Demonstrations calling for the defeat and destruction of America are a regular feature performance in the capitols of Khartoum and Tehran. Sudan's Popular Defense Forces, the militia to which most civilians belong, is organized around the concept of *jihad* or holy war against America[44]. Chants such as "*Jihad*, victory, martyrdom" and "Death to America! God is great!" are commonplace militia slogans[45]. Everyone from schoolchildren to college students and workers are taught by the Sudanese regime to hate the West[46].

Iran too, has found that preaching *jihad* against America and the West is a useful centerpiece of both its foreign and domestic policy. Iran's expansionist foreign policy is founded ultimately upon its constitution which states that the nation is committed "to perpetuate the [Islamic] revolution both at home and abroad."[47] In Tehran, the anniversary of the takeover of the American embassy in 1979 is celebrated annually with parades, speeches and demonstrations. In a very real sense then, as these examples make clear, America and the West are not yet at war with fundamentalist Islam but fundamentalist Islam is *already* at war with America and the West.

Islamic and Arabic insecurity about its standing in relation to the West occasionally has also displayed itself in a more bizarre way. In the 1980s, Libyan dictator Col. Khadaffi publicly asserted that William Shakespeare was really a Muslim and an Arab. Most Westerners quickly dismissed Khadaffi's speech as yet another indication of the Libyan leader's eccentricity and possible insanity. Yet, there is more to this story than that.

Khadaffi's assertion is highly significant because it reveals the extreme stresses that Western civilization has placed upon the Muslim psyche. From the context, it is obvious that Khadaffi and his audience felt threatened and intimidated by the fact that the Muslim world cannot claim this great writer as their own. Left with no option but to admit defeat or to stretch the truth about Arab and Islamic greatness, Khadaffi decided to weave his own myth on behalf of his people. As the Muslim Third World is increasingly confronted by the West's material, scientific and technological achievements at the end of the Cold War, such stresses and emotions will only increase.

Today there is great potential for a substantial increase in the Islamic world's hostility toward the West. Radical Islam's insecurity about its own place in the world, an insecurity that has typically expressed itself as hostility toward the West for reminding it of its own shortcomings, has always risen or fallen in proportion to Western fortunes. The apparent triumph of Western values and institutions at the end of the Cold War can only be interpreted as a challenge to Islam to define an alternative Islamic world order or be forced to fall in line with Western values and political and economic ideals.

Ominously, the followers of Islam see the world in only two shades. There is the nation of Islam, known as *dar al-Islam*, which encompasses all believers regardless of where they may reside[48]. *Dar al-Islam* may be thought of as a sort of loosely constituted Islamic super-state, if you will. Every place else in the world is known as *dar al-harb*, the domain of war, which should give one a chilling idea of Islam's longstanding hostility toward and perception of all non-Islamic peoples. According to tradition, between the two domains there can be an uneasy truce but no lasting peace[49]. *Jihad* or holy war against nonbelievers must break out eventually.

Western politicians and policy makers would be wise to remember this ancient and deeply ingrained Islamic worldview.

V. Strange Bedfellows: Fundamentalist Islam and Democracy

Fundamentalist Islam and liberal democracy are fundamentally incompatible. As we have seen, in a true Muslim state as envisioned by today's radical fundamentalists, there can be no politics outside of religion. All political questions are ultimately religious questions since Islam prescribes a complete way of life for its adherents. The very name "Islam" means to surrender[50]. A Muslim is one who surrenders to God's will as expressed in the Koran and interpreted by the religious leadership. By implication, political dissent also constitutes religious dissent and brings down upon the dissenters' heads charges of blasphemy, apostasy and sin[51]. The punishment for these 'crimes' can be severe.   In such a setting, liberal democratic institutions simply cannot work.   This is yet another reason why the Islamic world and the West appear to be on a collision course.

The Muslim world does have a concept of consultation, known as *shura*[52]. However, *shura* is a far cry from democracy.   Traditional Muslim governments are theoretically obligated to consult with the governed about the policies they plan to undertake. However, in the end Muslim rulers are free to make up their own minds about what course of action to take. They are not obligated to listen to the people, even if the people unanimously disagree with the ruler's planned course of action. *Shura* is more of a courtesy gesture extended by a ruler to the people than it is a hard and fast democratic principle.   The difference between *shura* and democracy is evident to fundamentalist Muslims themselves. Algerian Muslim opposition leader Ali Belhadj stated in a speech at a mosque in Algiers "We will not barter *shura* for democracy ... it is Islam which has been the victim, as always, not democracy. We did not go to the ballot boxes for democracy."[53]

Another Islamic concept is *ijma*, which means consensus[54]. This merely means that God's earthly community will never agree upon an error. Arguments concerning the meaning of *ijma* can quickly become self-serving. Consensus does not necessarily mean that all citizens of a nation or community agree with an Islamic leader's actions, only that such a leader's actions were not contrary to God's will. Religious scholars can play an important role in this respect by conferring legitimacy upon a ruler's actions. The *ulama* might announce that certain political actions are in accordance with Allah's will as expressed in the Koran. By implication in this scenario, the suppression of dissidents who oppose the ruling regime's policies is morally acceptable because political dissent constitutes opposition to God's will. Once again, Islam finds itself unable to tolerate political dissent. Without political tolerance, a "loyal opposition" cannot exist and therefore democratic institutions cannot possibly take root.

Democratic ideals are also suspect in the Muslim world because they are viewed as "Western imports." Democracy is perceived as just another legacy of colonialism[55]. Thus, hostility toward the West also plays into the hands of those wishing to establish a radical religious dictatorship instead of a representative form of government. Unfortunately, democratic values cannot receive a warm reception in the Muslim world if native sources for such values cannot be eventually pointed out. Historically, some pro-Western reformers in the Islamic world have attempted to find Islamic roots for various Western ideas such as democracy, representative forms of government, capitalism, etc., in order to make those ideas more palatable to the *ulama* and the populace at large[56]. But there is no denying that democracy is a Western concept born of "a thousand years of European history, and beyond that by Europe's double heritage: Judeo-Christian religion and ethics; Greco-Roman statecraft and law."[57] Thus, democracy is as alien to the Islamic world as communism or socialism.

But the incompatibility between democracy on the one hand and the kind of government the radical Muslims seek to establish on the other has not prevented Muslim propagandists from cynically exploiting democratic rhetoric in order to mislead the public and to portray as bigotted alarmists those concerned about the growth of radical Islam. For example, fundamentalist leaders agitating for power in Algeria (under the banner of the Islamic Salvation Front) and in other states have been strong proponents of such staples of democracy as national elections primarily because they perceive national elections as the easiest way for them to come to power. Islamic activists have disingenuously asserted before the Western media and the media in their own countries that the fundamentalist Islamic regime they hope to establish in Algeria would be compatible with democratic values (e.g., political pluralism, tolerance, minority rights, women's rights, etc.)[58] However, looking at what these leaders do and not just at what they say for popular consumption, it quickly becomes evident that democratic elections are merely a tool for seizing power and not a dearly held ideal. As one prominent scholar, Bernard Lewis, recently stated:

> [Muslim fundamentalists] make no secret of their contempt for democratic political procedures...Their attitude toward democratic elections has been summed up as 'one man, one vote, once.'[59]

This attitude was clearly evident in Algeria's aborted national election. Before the Islamic Salvation Front ("FIS") won a plurality in Algeria's nationwide balloting in December, 1991, the FIS assuaged the fears of Algeria's Westernized middle class by adopting a tone of political moderation and promising an economic program that would spur prosperity for all[60]. At the same time, the group attacked the discredited and corrupt ruling elite and promised economic salvation to the masses of desperate poor. Having thereby secured the most votes of any political party in the December balloting, the Islamic Salvation Front quickly became convinced that it was moving toward inevitable victory in the second run-off round of elections. The group quickly shed the moderate and accommodating image it had assiduously cultivated and sternly stated that when they took power there would be no national constitution or legal code other than God's law as written in the Koran itself[61]. Many feared that if national elections had not been cancelled by a subsequent military coup, this fundamentalist group would have been the last beneficiary of elections in modern day Algeria.

VI. Fundamentalist Islam and Capitalism

The traditional Muslim world in many ways occupies the position of medieval Europe when it comes to attitudes toward capitalism and commercial enterprise. In Europe during the Middle Ages banking and commerce were generally looked upon with disfavor by the ruling elite. Business was not only looked upon as an unworthy activity in a sociological sense; it was also perceived negatively in a religious and ethical sense as well. Thus, in medieval Europe marginalized groups like the Jews were relegated to such tasks as money lending (which later grew into banking) and the like. The nobility's religious objections to commercial, and particularly banking, activities sprung from a supposed Biblical injunction against charging interest on loans and profiting from another's labor.

The Muslims, particularly the ultra-conservative fundamentalists, are in a very similar situation today. The Muslim prohibition against *riba* or charging interest, makes most modern, large scale commercial activities problematic[62]. This religious prohibition springs from chapter 3, verse 10 of the Koran which states "Believers! Do not live on interest, doubled and redoubled!" Out goes the banking industry and possibly insurance and financial services as well! Paralleling medieval Europe's use of the Jewish community for such tasks, the Muslim world over the centuries has similarly looked to non-Muslim groups like the Jews and also the Christians including the Greeks and Armenians to handle such commercial tasks[63].

But this is where the similarities end. In Florence and Venice, Bruges in present day Belgium, and elsewhere on the European continent, the West was eventually able to put its excessively rigid religious interpretations aside. An expanding middle class founded capital stock companies, banking houses and a primitive insurance industry with which to launch, fund and underwrite large scale commercial ventures. Commercial activity in the West eventually led to Columbus' voyage to America and countless other voyages of discovery in search of material wealth during the fifteenth and sixteenth centuries. Capitalism had plainly taken root throughout Europe by this time.

In contrast to Christian Europe, the Muslims still looked askance at commercial activities. Consequently they, like the introspective Chinese who had a similar view of commerce and all things Western, fell further and further behind the West in terms of wealth, military and political power and technological advancement. Even today, the Muslim world must tiptoe around the prohibition against *riba*. Muslims accomplish this in a number of ways[64]. First, *riba* might be interpreted as an injunction against usury not interest. Usury, of course, is an inordinately high rate of interest. Thus, one might argue that the Koran only prohibits usurious rates of interest. Another technique is for banks to charge a "service fee" on loans instead of interest. A service fee of three percent has been common in the Muslim world lately. Such a low fee can be defended as a bona fide service fee or, alternatively, as an acceptably low rate of interest which is not usurious.

Muslims have also structured their corporate arrangements in still other ways to get around the Koran's prohibition. Under a practice known as *murabaha*, a lending bank actually takes title of the subject of the loan (say a piece of machinery that is being purchased) during the term of the loan. The borrower meanwhile has free use of the machinery, property or whatever the borrower purchased with the money loaned by the bank. At the end of the loan period, title is transferred to the borrower and the borrower pays the bank an additional sum above and beyond the face amount of the loan in gratitude for the bank serving as the owner of the item during the period of the loan.

Still another means of avoiding the prohibition against *riba* involves practices known as *mudaraba* and *musharaka*. Under these closely related practices the bank acts as an investor in, not a lender to, a particular enterprise, sharing the risk of loss or eventual gain depending on the ultimate outcome of the venture. The attractiveness of this approach is that financial institutions have even more of an incentive to closely scrutinize the companies they invest in. The downside is that they may face lawsuits or mass withdrawals from depositors whose savings and retirement money have been placed at risk.

In short, the traditional Muslim world can tolerate with some difficulty the existence of commercial activities including banking, insurance and financial services. But official toleration by the Islamic fundamentalists is a narrowly circumscribed affair. Capitalist ventures operate under tight constraints in the Muslim world and are viewed with some amount of hostility and suspicion by the *ulama*. Iran's suffocating atmosphere is no place for commerce on a Western scale. President Rafsanjani has hoped to overcome this problem however, by turning two Iranian islands, Kish Island and Qeshm Island, into shopping meccas[65]. Shops on the two islands stay open throughout the holy month of Ramadan and limited sales of alcohol are tolerated. The islands are also the beneficiaries of an investment code designed to favor commercial development. Religious leaders in Tehran's parliament, the *majles*, are unhappy over these developments but have been thwarted for the moment. Kish and Qeshm underscore the fact that fundamentalist Islamic values are indeed a significant roadblock to commercial development and economic integration with the rest of the world. One must literally move offshore to engage in capitalist activity in the fundamentalist Muslim world. But the islands also demonstrate that there are ways in which proto-capitalist elements within the fundamentalist Muslim world can overcome such obstacles, albeit with some difficulty.

VII. Fundamentalist Islam and Human Rights

A. In General

Universal human rights generally have not been widely respected and observed by Islamic fundamentalist regimes. In Sudan, political dissidents, secularists, socialists and other free thinkers who do not tow the radical Islamic line are often taken into custody by the Sudanese military, tortured and detained in various "ghost houses" around Khartoum[66]. Many disappear permanently. In 1993 Amnesty International accused Sudan of gross human rights violations including the "ethnic cleansing" of the Nuba people located in southern Sudan[67]. Iran under the mullahs has a similarly abysmal record on human rights[68]. The Shah's dreaded secret service, SAVAK, has been replaced by the equally dreaded VEVAK (the Ministry of Intelligence and Security or Vezarat-e Etela'at va Amniyat-e Keshvar) of the Islamic militants. The Islamic Republic of Iran gets rid of its dissidents by bringing them to trial on various bizarre or trumped up legal charges. For example, political opponents have been accused of "siding with global arrogance" (the radical Muslims' all-inclusive phrase for siding with the West in some manner), "moral corruption," or engaging in "anti-revolutionary behavior."[69] Opponents have also been summarily executed and their cause discredited after being falsely accused by the authorities of drug smuggling and the like[70].

The revolutionary court system in Iran aids and abets the regime in its effort to rid the nation of opponents. Political cases are tried by special courts[71]. Defense lawyers are not allowed, and defendants have no right to appeal their sentence[72]. Sometimes a single mullah will sit in judgment of a capital case for an alleged political crime[73]. In short, justice in Iran is hard to come by. Like Stalinist Russia during the Great Purges of the 1930s, the fundamentalist Muslims run a kangaroo court system where political opponents are routinely imprisoned, tortured or murdered after undergoing a show trial, the outcome of which is never in doubt.

Journalists, writers and artists in the Islamic Republic of Iran face a similar ordeal if their work is deemed offensive to Muslim sensibilities. Artists must adhere to special aesthetic guidelines issued by the Ministry of Islamic Guidance or face prison[74]. Journalists also face imprisonment or worse if they write stories that are deemed "'damaging to the revolution.'"[75] Free expression and honest discourse on the issues of the day are not tolerated inside the Islamic Republic of Iran.

Both nations have been the subject of scathing reports by Amnesty International, the United States State Department and the United Nations for violating the human rights of their citizens. The United Nations special representative on human rights, Reynaldo Galindo-Pohl, has not even been allowed inside Iran since 1991[76]. In 1992, the Iranian press stopped publishing the names of those executed by the government when the fundamentalist regime realized that the West was keeping track of human rights abuses by recording the death tally[77].

Predictably, the Iranians have scoffed at international criticism and concern for human rights inside their country. The fundamentalist Muslim response to international criticism of their human rights record essentially consists of several counter-charges. Muslims are merely imposing "Islamic values" on their own people. The West is culturally arrogant if it thinks that its definition of human rights is the only definition or the "international" one. Muslims also falsely accuse the West of persecuting Islam whenever any international human rights group raises a concern about this or that writer being tortured, killed or having a price put on his head. Iranian foreign minister Ali Akbar Velayati's recent statement reflects fundamentalist thinking concerning human rights:

> Human rights in Iran are based on Islamic values... We will not accept the values of foreign countries imposed on us under the cover of human rights[78].

One strongly suspects that Westerners and Islamists are talking past one another when they speak of human rights. The reader will notice that Velayati plainly prefers the term "Islamic values" and only grudgingly uses the term "human rights" because he feels it is constantly being foisted upon his country by Western nations and international institutions like the United Nations. When the West speaks of human rights it refers to a set of fundamental rights enjoyed by all of humanity that cannot be legitimately revoked or trampled upon by any state. These rights are at their source "natural rights" in the Lockean sense of the term, meaning that they existed when humanity theoretically was still in a state of nature before the founding of any state. The preexistence of these fundamental rights is the primary reason they take precedence over the wishes of a state. (Another reason is that such rights have through their prevalence worldwide become enshrined as customary international law.)

In contrast, in "[t]raditional Islam" there is "no doctrine of human rights, the very notion of which might seem an impiety. Only God has rights - human beings have duties."[79] Thus, the clash between Islam and the West on the issue of basic human rights is at heart nothing less than a clash between fundamentally different views of the individual and the state. To the radical Muslims, individuals have no inherent rights other than what God grants. As for the concept of the state in radical Islam, religious and political power are one. Ideally, the state in Islamic theory is nothing more than the community of believers or *ummah*. Because the Islamic nation is God's community on earth, the state's enemies are by implication God's enemies. Political opposition in a traditional Muslim theocracy therefore constitutes opposition to God[80]. Such opposition is an act of apostasy. The penalty for apostasy is death. Death or anything less than death such as imprisonment or torture is therefore theoretically and rhetorically acceptable to fundamentalist Muslims who view themselves as merely carrying out God's law concerning unbelievers.

As for Lockean rights, fundamentalist Muslims would view the whole concept of natural rights which pre-exist and are superior to nation-states as arrogant. How can human beings have rights which are superior to God's nation of believers, a nation with laws that represent His will? To the fundamentalists, the West's insistence upon certain internationally recognized human rights represents an attempt to place the rights and privileges of human beings above God. This, in some small part, is what the Iranian revolutionary government means when it refers to the West's "global arrogance" or when it calls America "the Great Satan" since Satan was the one who attempted to place himself above God's will.

These profound philosophical differences have been expressed in other ways as well. In the realm of public international law countries like the Islamic Republic of Iran have attempted to go their own way in defining legal rights and duties which are at odds with virtually the rest of the world. For example, there are currently 117 countries that are signatories to the International Covenant on Civil and Political Rights which includes the right to freedom of expression, freedom from torture, slavery, arbitrary arrest and detention, and many other rights[81]. Most nations of the world have also signed the Universal Declaration of Human Rights[82], a multi-lateral treaty that was largely created in response to the horrors of World War II and the atrocities committed by the Nazis and the Imperial Japanese. Since its creation in 1948, the Universal Declaration of Human Rights has become the bedrock of modern human rights law.

Fundamentalist Muslim leaders have rejected these world conventions and instead have sought to construct their own vision of the rights of the individual and the state. Their blueprint was embodied in 1981 in an Islamic Declaration of Human Rights which was purportedly written in accordance with the *sharia* and which circumscribed or completely omitted several of the basic rights found in the former covenants. Basic human rights like the right to freely choose one's own spouse and freedom from forced child marriages are recognized by the world community in Article 16 of the Universal Declaration of Rights. These rights are not recognized by the fundamentalist Muslim countries because the *sharia* permits child marriage and allows families, particularly fathers, to play a deciding role in deciding whether and whom their children will marry. Article 18's guarantee of freedom of thought and religion is at odds with Islam's rule that those who convert from Islam to another religion including Christianity can be put to death. Article 19 of the Universal Declaration of Rights provides that "[e]veryone has the right to freedom of opinion and expression." Salman Rushdie and many other writers, dissidents and intellectuals are routinely threatened with death, torture and imprisonment by fundamentalist Muslim regimes for speaking their mind. Islamic states do not permit let alone guarantee free speech when the content of such speech is deemed "un-Islamic" or otherwise contrary to the tenets of Islam.

Philosophical differences make it somewhat difficult to find a common vocabulary for speaking about human rights. The fundamentalist Muslim world and the West have almost diametrically opposed visions of the individual and the state. Cultural frictions and resentments are part of the equation as well. The Muslim world views Western criticism of its human rights record as a manifestation of the West's cultural arrogance. Even the United Nations' efforts in this regard are viewed with hostility and suspicion since the United Nations is widely perceived as an instrument of the United States and Western Europe, despite the fact that China and Russia sit on the U.N. Security Council. Admittedly, public international law which forms the basis of human rights complaints against the Muslim countries is to a significant degree an expression of Western concepts and ideas of one sort or another which have taken root worldwide.

Yet if the burden of proof were placed on the radical Muslims, they would be hard pressed to find express support in the Koran for Iran's and Sudan's terror tactics against their own people. The Koran counsels respect for human life, not torture. Foreign minister Velayati's assertion that Iran is merely imposing Islamic values is not entirely accurate. Iran is doing nothing of the sort when it executes writers, artists, journalists and opposition politicians without due process on trumped up charges. Those are the cold-blooded tactics of a ruthless dictatorship. Such acts are unworthy of one of the world's great monotheistic religions. When all is said and done there is, or should be, a least common denominator concerning the minimum standards by which all nations must treat their citizens, whether they are civilians, dissidents or prisoners. Surely both the Western nations and the fundamentalist Muslims can agree on minimum standards for the physical treatment of such unfortunates.

B. The Attack on Women's Rights

The inferior status of women in fundamentalist Islamic countries represents another friction point between the Islamic world and the West. Equality between the sexes was one of the major social revolutions of the 20th century. The revolution in women's rights culminated in the United States and Europe largely in the 1960s and 70s. It has yet to occur in fundamentalist Islamic countries[83]. In fact, since the mullahs seized power in Iran, equality for women as a societal goal seems further out of reach than ever. Whenever and wherever the radical Muslims have taken power, the personal status of women has suffered a comparative decline. Women's rights are significantly restricted in traditional Muslim societies and would continue to be further circumscribed if the fundamentalist revolution now found in Iran and Sudan continues to spread.

The inferior status of women stems directly from the Koran and the *sharia*, the Islamic legal code governing domestic relations. Verse 34 of Chapter 4 of the Koran quotes God as saying that men "have authority" over women[84]. This phrase is open to some interpretation. Other phrases are not. For "disloyalty and ill-conduct," the Koran authorizes husbands to take several steps to correct the situation[85]: First, husbands should "admonish" their wives which is interpreted as a verbal scolding of some sort. Second, if that does not work, God advises husbands in the Koran to "refuse to share their beds." The third option is for husbands to "beat them." Islamists of various stripes have argued about the number of blows but never the fact that striking one's wife is permissible in God's eyes according to the Koran. Amazingly, progressive Islamists argue that this last phrase refers only to a single blow[86]. No one has apparently yet put forth a credible argument that the Koran does not countenance physical violence against women at all. Some have attempted to argue that the verb "to strike" in the Koran really means to impress upon wives the error of their ways through force of argument alone but this interpretation seems somewhat far-fetched[87].

Islamic law contains other provisions which place women in a substantially inferior status compared to men. In Iran, child marriage is permitted. Soon after coming to power, Ayatollah Khomeini reduced the legal marriage age for women from eighteen to nine[88]. Polygamy has also been restored. According to fundamentalist religious leaders, the Koran allows a Muslim man to have 4 wives while women are restricted to 1 husband[89]. In the case of a virgin female, the woman's invariably male guardian has an unqualified right to marry her to whomever he wishes[90].

The Koran's decrees concerning divorce are also lopsided[91]. A man can obtain an immediate divorce merely by orally reciting a declaration of repudiation three times. This may be as simple as saying "I divorce you, I divorce you, I divorce you." In contrast, a woman generally needs to obtain the consent of her husband if she wants a divorce (an unlikely scenario if the man does not feel similarly). The divorced wife must then wait a certain amount of time before being permitted to remarry and may also lose custody of her children. Child custody laws in general favor men[92]. Boys older than two and girls older than seven belong exclusively to their fathers. In the settlement of an estate, under the *sharia* a daughter inherits only half the amount of a son. In court, a woman's testimony counts only half as much as a man's testimony[93]. Clearly, the position of women under traditional Islamic law in fundamentalist Islamic countries is significantly inferior to men.

The oppression of women in traditional and fundamentalist Muslim societies is reinforced by battalions of police and legions of semi-official gangs of young males who roam the streets harassing and terrorizing female pedestrians and shoppers. These semi-official gangs, known as the *komiteh*, are the self-appointed guardians of a woman's morality and manner of dress[94]. Women are challenged or detained for not wearing proper Islamic dress, such as the full body length chador and a veil over the face. Women are also rudely checked for signs of makeup, perfume and nail polish. Offenders can be arrested and imprisoned. Punishments can range from a fine to a whipping. Couples are also harassed by the *komiteh* if they are seen engaging in "un-Islamic behavior" which can cover everything from holding hands, walking too closely to one another or kissing.

In Iran, the fines, abuse, beatings, imprisonment and petty harassment of women have gotten so bad that many highly educated and intelligent women have been essentially forced out of the work force[95]. One professional woman stated bitterly:

> I wanted to do my work and do it well...But all the time I was worrying who will report this conversation, can they see my hair, did I get rid of the smell of the perfume from last night?[96]

An American-educated doctor who returned to her native Iran reflected on her decision to give up practising medicine:

> The energy I used arguing about the way I dressed, the way I talked, my refusal to stop to pray and a million other things that had nothing to do with curing the sick, was making me sick[97].

The plight of women living in fundamentalist Muslim countries, particularly of female professionals who have been unable to lead productive work lives because of harassment from male office colleagues, is a tragedy of epic proportions.

The penalties for women who break traditional Islamic law are severe and barbaric by current international standards. For example according to published reports, in April, 1991 alone Iran punished 800 women with 74 lashes each for not wearing a veil[98]. There have been many other reports of the trials and hardships women face in attempting to function with any semblance of dignity in Iran and elsewhere under the Islamic fundamentalists.

In the largely Muslim country of Bangladesh, local unofficial bodies consisting of village elders and local Islamic clerics have enforced traditional Islamic values and standards at the village and town level. These local councils, known as the *shalish*, have ruthlessly applied the Koran and other conservative Muslim standards to women. A *shalish* in Bangladesh condemned twenty-one year old Noorjahan Begum to death by stoning because she had recently married again even though her first husband alleged that they were not officially divorced[99]. A sixteen year old girl named Feroza died after being publicly flogged for having intercourse with a Hindu boy[100]. Fourteen year old Zulekha Begum passed out after receiving 74 of the 101 lashes a local *shalish* ordered as her punishment for allegedly having sex with a married man from the next village[101]. Despite the fact that she was a minor, local leaders apparently did not inquire whether the man had enticed her to have sex with him. The focus of the inquiry and the subsequent punishment was directed exclusively at the girl. Dozens of other incidents have been reported across the country.

The gulf between the international women's rights movement and fundamentalist Islam's conception of a woman's rights and role in society is indeed great. It is troubling and repulsive to see Iran, Sudan and radical fundamentalist (as opposed to moderate) Muslims in other countries defend their barbaric treatment of women as merely their way of expressing and preserving an Islamic woman's "dignity." There is nothing dignified about the incidents mentioned above. The brutal suppression, torture and killing of women in these countries resembles nothing more than a campaign of religious terrorism directed against women.

The disparity between Western and fundamentalist Muslim views of equality between the sexes is substantial and constitutes yet another source of friction between the two societies. It is almost impossible to reconcile the two points of view. The Muslims point to the Koran itself for their behavior. It is fruitless to argue against the primacy of the Koran or the *sharia* with fundamentalists. At most, one can only encourage more moderate interpretations of certain troubling provisions of chapter 4 of the Koran which seem to clearly approve of physical violence against women within the marital relationship.

Some have argued that the treatment of women in traditional Muslim societies springs more from historical and cultural conditions than it does from Islam itself[102]. It is true that Islam sprang from a nomadic society in which women were considered inferior to men. Unfortunately this early nomadic tradition of inequality between the sexes was reflected in what the Prophet said and did while alive and therefore was rapidly embodied in the early Islamic legal codes of the time. It is also true that Islam absorbed some of the culture of the territories it conquered. For example, ladies of leisure in Syria wore veils. This manner of dress was adopted by the conquering Arabic Empire. The Persians also treated women as inferior to men. The Muslims assimilated such attitudes when they absorbed Persia. But no one can deny the Koran and the *sharia* as sources of women's inferiority to men in traditional Muslim societies. The religious passages and laws quoted or referred to above cannot be dismissed as merely a reflection of social attitudes. Inequality between the sexes appears to be a central part of the Muslim religion. It will not be easy to overcome.

C. The Attack on Other Religions

Muslims don't always tolerate the existence of other religions very well. This is evident in the vocabulary they use to describe nonbelievers. Those who are not Muslims are referred to as inhabiting the domain of war, *dar al-harb*[103]. Thus, Muslims automatically take an adversarial posture toward the rest of the entire world. With the radical fundamentalists, the situation is even worse. Muslims are rhetorically and often literally ready to go to war against all nonbelievers. This zeal for warfare with non-Muslims extends to their domestic policies as well. Christians have been imprisoned, tortured, shot, bombed and executed by fundamentalist Muslim nations simply because they were Christians. In Iran, a Protestant Bishop named Haik Hovsepian Mehr, age 49, was recently killed by Iranian authorities after he brought international attention to the case of a 60 year old Iranian man, Mehdi Dibaj, who was sentenced to death by the Iranian Government merely for converting from Islam to Christianity[104]. Under Islamic law apostasy, including converting to another religion from Islam, is punishable by death. Bishop Mehr's efforts succeeded in embarassing Tehran, and the man was released. Soon afterwards though, Bishop Mehr was cruelly kidnapped by Iranian security forces, stabbed to death and later secretly buried in a Muslim cemetery by the Iranian government. Bishop Mehr's family eventually learned of his fate and received permission from the government to exhume the body and bury it in a Christian cemetery.

Christians in fundamentalist Iran are closely watched. State security forces attend church services to make sure Christians aren't evangelizing the local Muslim community. Those caught evangelizing can be put to death. It is also illegal to translate the Bible into Persian.

Other sects are vigorously persecuted by the Iranian government as well. Members of the Bahai faith are periodically tortured, imprisoned or executed by the Islamic Republic of Iran even though Iranian authorities maintain that other religions are not persecuted in any way. Recently, the twelve year old daughter of a Bahai leader from Tehran was purportedly kidnapped and tortured by the Iranian government in an effort to intimidate members of the Bahai faith in Iran[105]. In December, 1993 three Bahai adherents were sentenced to death by Iran for their faith in violation of international law[106]. They were accused of holding a Bahai religious feast and of the bizarrely worded crime of being "unprivileged infidels at war with the Muslim nation."[107]

The Islamic Republic of Iran's persecution of those of other faiths as a matter of state policy stands in stark contrast to a basic tenet of Western political thought. The influential seventeenth century political philosopher John Locke stated in 1689:

> [N]either Pagan nor Mahometan, nor Jew, ought to be ex-
> cluded from the civil rights of the commonwealth because of
> his religion[108].

The Sudanese government similarly harasses, intimidates and kills members of its Christian community. Conditions for Christians were so bad in Sudan, particularly in the southern provinces where Christians have become the victims of state-sponsored genocide, that Pope John Paul II courageously chastised that country in a public speech while visiting Khartoum. Pope John Paul II in particular has worked tirelessly to bridge the gap of understanding between Muslims and Christians and to promote harmony and tolerance between the two faiths. In his recent bestselling book *Crossing The Threshold Of Hope*, His Holiness stated that "'[t]he Church has a high regard for the Muslims'" and recounts the Roman Catholic Church's attempts to have a dialogue with members of that "*great monotheistic*" faith[109]. The Pope recalled the numerous pastoral trips he has made to Africa, Asia and the Middle East to meet with Muslim religious and secular leaders and the prayer session he held at Assisi, Italy for the Muslim victims of genocide in Bosnia[110]. But even the Pope finds the hostile and uncompromising stance of the fundamentalist Muslims difficult to overcome.

> Nevertheless, concrete difficulties are not lacking. In countries where fundamentalist movements come to power, human rights and the principle of religious freedom are unfortunately interpreted in a very one-sided way - religious freedom comes to mean freedom to impose on all citizens the "true religion." In these countries the situation of Christians is sometimes terribly disturbing. Fundamentalist attitudes of this nature make reciprocal contacts very difficult. All the same, the Church remains always open to dialogue and cooperation[111].

Christian-Muslim relations, particularly with the radical, fundamentalist branch of Islam, have deteriorated despite the best efforts of the Christian community to reach some kind of understanding that would enable those of both faiths to live without fear in one another's midst.

Conditions in Egypt have also gotten worse for Christians. In smaller towns and rural areas, Muslim activists have targeted and killed Christians as a matter of policy[112]. Islamic scholars and university academics in Egypt have distributed hundreds of taped speeches calling on Muslims to shun their Christian brethren[113]. Sheik Omar Abdelkalfi stated on one tape that Muslims should not walk on the same sidewalk or shake hands with Christians. Nor should Muslims wish Christians well on Christian holidays, according to Sheik Abdelkalfi. This call for segregating and isolating Christian citizens reveals the pathological hatred, bigotry and intolerance that some fundamentalist Muslims have for those of other faiths. Coupled with acts of violence against Christians, the espousal of such policies is reminiscent of the early anti-Jewish laws passed by Hitler's Reichstag in the 1930s. Fundamentalist Islamic attitudes toward Judaism and the existence of Israel, of course, need no explanation. The radical Muslims are fanatical in their hatred of both.

D. The Attack on Freedom of Expression

The Islamic Republic of Iran's *fatwa* or death edict against British citizen and author Salman Rushdie which was issued on February 14, 1989 underscores the fundamentalist Muslim world's total disregard for Mr. Rushdie's rights under international law and demonstrates fundamentalist Islam's increasing intolerance and hostility toward the West. Mr. Rushdie's right to freedom of expression under Article 19 of the International Covenant of Civil and Political Rights was plainly violated by Iran's death sentence. Article 19 of the Covenant on Civil and Political Rights reads in part:

> Everyone shall have the right to hold opinions without interference...Everyone shall have the right to freedom of expression; this right shall include freedom to seek, receive and impart information and ideas of all kinds, regardless of frontiers, either orally, in writing or in print, in the form of art, or through any other media of his choice[114].

While done in the name of Islam, the manner in which Khomeini issued the death sentence against Salman Rushdie actually contravened several Islamic legal rules and principles[115]. According to the *sharia*, accused apostates have the right to recant their alleged apostasy. Mr. Rushdie was not allowed such a right before Khomeini issued his international contract for the murder of Rushdie. In addition, the Iranian leader rebuffed the author's attempts to recant and stated that the death sentence could never be lifted even if Mr. Rushdie became the most pious Muslim of his time. The death sentence is also legally extraordinary in several other respects including the offer of a multimillion dollar bounty to anyone in the world who executes the sentence, the sentencing by a Shia cleric of someone who is a member of the Sunni faith and who therefore falls outside of the jurisdiction of a Shia religious court, and the lack of due process (even by Islamic standards) afforded to Mr. Rushdie generally. The extra-jurisdictional aspects of the affair are also extraordinary since traditional Islamic law allows rulers jurisdiction only over those within its geographic territory. Mr. Rushdie is a British citizen who had not set foot inside Iran. In sum, the Rushdie affair is hardly legal under either international law or most interpretations of Islamic law. Nonetheless, Iran was able to persuade the Organization of Islamic Conference to characterize Rushdie's book as blasphemous and to label the writer himself an apostate[116]. Iran has steadfastly defended its decision and has refused to debate the legality of the *fatwa* under Islamic law. In effect, Iran seems to be saying that any action it takes is, by definition, legal under the tenets of Islam because Iran is an Islamic nation. This is a rather circular, self-supporting and spurious line of reasoning and indicates the enormous challenges faced by anyone attempting to have an honest intellectual debate with fundamentalist Muslims on this issue.

The entire affair demonstrates the radical Islamic world's profound hostility toward free expression (a Western value) generally and Great Britain, America and the West in particular. The incident has mobilized domestic support for the radical Muslims who have portrayed themselves as the defenders of Islam against its critics, and has polarized the Islamic and Western worlds.

Mr. Rushdie is not the first intellectual and certainly will not be the last to be threatened by the fundamentalists. Ms. Taslima Nasrin, a doctor and novelist from Bangladesh, is yet another writer who has been threatened with death for questioning certain aspects of Islam[117]. She has fled her country and remains in hiding while fundamentalist Islamic groups repeat calls for her to be killed.

An earlier, less well-known incident involved a political and religious theorist in Sudan named Mahmud Muhammad Taha. Taha advocated a more moderate interpretation of Islam that was at odds with the Nimeiri regime which held power in Sudan at the time[118]. In January, 1985 Taha was arrested, tried and sentenced to die as an apostate under Islamic law.

Taha was hung on January 18, 1985 at the age of 76. The Nimeiri regime, though short-lived (1983-85), demonstrated the wrath that fundamentalists have for those who disagree with their strict interpretation of the Koran and the *sharia*. Taha was merely a representative of the liberal wing of Islam. He did not deny the essential truth of the religion (the essence of apostasy) so much as argue in favor of a more moderate interpretation of its tenets. Applying radical Muslim arguments in favor of executing Rushdie and Nasrin to the West generally, all of Western society in a sense is an "enemy of Islam" in fundamentalist eyes because it endorses freedom of intellectual and artistic expression and permits the kind of criticism (including self-criticism) that fundamentalists abhor. Through acts of murder, attempted murder, torture, imprisonment and terrorism, the fundamentalists have essentially declared war on Western civilization[119].

§ § §

ENDNOTES

1.   Phillips, "Saddamization of Iran," 6; Lewis, "Islam And Liberal Democracy," *The Atlantic Monthly*, 89, 91 (February, 1993).

2.   "A world terrorist link?" *The Hartford Courant*, C1 (Sunday, June 20, 1993).

3.   Islamic Republic News Agency (IRNA), July 18, 1990.

4.   Nixon, *SEIZE THE MOMENT: America's Challenge in A One-Superpower World*, 195. Another source states that the number is 800 million. *The Statesman's Yearbook 1992-93*, Brian Hunter ed. *The World Almanac and Book of Facts 1994* places this number at over 971 million as of mid-1992. See *World Almanac and Book of Facts 1994*, 722. Robert Famighetti et. al. eds. The well-respected British newsmagazine *The Economist* says the total is 1.2 billion. "Islam And The West," *The Economist*, 18 (August 6-12, 1994).

5.   See *The Statesman's yearbook 1992-93* and *The World Almanac and Book of Facts 1994.*

6.   Wright, "Islam, Democracy and the West," 131, 139; Kaplan, "Shatter Zone," *The Atlantic Monthly*, 24, 24-25 (April, 1992); see also Taheri, *Crescent in a Red Sky: The Future Of Islam In The Soviet Union*, 121.

7.   Ibid.

8.   For a detailed description of the origins and early history of Islam, see Mortimer, *Faith & Power: The Politics of Islam*, 15-49.

9.   Mortimer, *Faith & Power*, 34, 80.

10.   Ibid.

11.   Mortimer, *Faith & Power*, 34.

12.   Mortimer, *Faith & Power*, 36.

13.   Mortimer, *Faith & Power*, 36-37.

14.   Mortimer, *Faith & Power*, 56-57; *The Cambridge Encyclopedia of the Middle East and North Africa*, 196-215, 224-275; Kennedy, *The Rise and Fall Of The Great Powers*, 10-11.

15.   Kennedy, *Rise and Fall of the Great Powers*, 10-11.

16.   Kennedy, *Rise and Fall of the Great Powers*, 10.

17.   Kennedy, *Rise and Fall of the Great Powers*, 9-10; Lewis, *The Emergence of Modern Turkey*, 23-26.

18.   Lewis, *The Emergence of Modern Turkey*, 23-26.

19.   Ibid; Kennedy, *Rise and Fall of the Great Powers*, 11-12.

20.   Lewis, *The Emergence of Modern Turkey*, 23-239, Pfaff, *THE WRATH OF NATIONS*, 97.

21. Lewis, *The Emergence of Modern Turkey*, 238-241.

22. Kennedy, *Rise and Fall of the Great Powers*, 9-13.

23. Ibid.

24. Ibid.

25. See generally Mortimer, *Faith & Power*, 15-49.

26. Ibid.; *The Cambridge Encyclopedia*, 166-169.

27. *The Cambridge Encyclopedia*, 166-169; Wright, "Islam and Democracy," 133; Miller, "The Challenge of Radical Islam," 42, 50-51.

28. Lewis, "Islam And Liberal Democracy," *The Atlantic Monthly*, 89, 91 (February, 1993).

29. *The Cambridge Encyclopedia*, 181.

30. "Islam And The West," *The Economist*, 3, 9 (August 6-12, 1994).

31. See generally Mortimer, *Faith & Power*, 39-55.

32. Wright, "Islam and Democracy," 132.

33. Mortimer, *Faith & Power*, 44-45; Pfaff, *THE WRATH OF NATIONS*, 141.

34. See generally Safran, *Israel: The Embattled Ally*.

35. See Lewis, "Islam And Liberal Democracy."

36. Wright, "New Breed of Terrorist Worries U.S.," *Los Angeles Times*, A5, A7 (June 28, 1993).

37. See generally Lewis, *The Emergence of Modern Turkey*, 21-209; Pfaff, *THE WRATH OF NATIONS*, 119-128.

38. Lewis, *The Emergence of Modern Turkey*, 268-270.

39. E.L. Jones, *The European Miracle: Environments, Economies and Geopolitics in the History of Europe and Asia*, 182.

40. Kennedy, *The Rise and Fall of the Great Powers*, 12.

41. Lewis, *The Emergence of Modern Turkey*, 21-209.

42. Ibid.

43. See e.g., Lewis, *The Emergence of Modern Turkey*, 83.

44. "Jihad," *The Economist*, 42-43 (August 7-13, 1993).

45. Ibid.

46. Ibid.

47. "Constitution of the Islamic Republic of Iran," *Middle East Journal*, 34 (1980): 185.

48. *The Cambridge Encyclopedia*, 167.

49. Ibid.

50. Mortimer, *Faith & Power*, 32.

51. Lewis, "Islam and Liberal Democracy," 96.

52. "Islam And The West," *The Economist*, 12-13 (August 6-12, 1994).

53. *Le Monde*, June 17-18, 1990, as quoted in E.G.H. Joffe, "Relations Between the Middle East and the West," *Middle East Journal* 48, no. 2 (Spring 1994): 250, 260, footnote 26.

54. Ibid.

55. Korany, "Arab Democratization: A Poor Cousin?," 511-513.

56. Lewis, "Islam and Liberal Democracy," 90; Lewis, *The Emergence of Modern Turkey*, 142.

57. Lewis, "Islam and Liberal Democracy," 93.

58. Miller, "The Challenge of Radical Islam," 43, 48.

59. Lewis, "Islam and Liberal Democracy," 91; see also Sivan, "Eavesdropping on Radical Islam," 13, 21.

60. Miller, "The Challenge of Radical Islam," 48.

61. Ibid.

62. "Islam and the West," *The Economist*, 9 (August 6-12, 1994).

63. Pfaff, *THE WRATH OF NATIONS*, 92-93.

64. Ibid.

65. "Free for all, but keep your veil on," *The Economist*, 46 (September 10-16, 1994).

66. See Langewiesche, "Turabi's Law," *The Atlantic Monthly*, 26, 29, 32-33 (August, 1994); "Rest camp for terrorists," *The Economist*, 48 (September 17-23, 1994); Miller, "The Challenge of Radical Islam," 43, 48.

67. *The World Almanac and Book of Facts 1994*, 811.

68. "Walk in fear," *The Economist*, 39-40 (July 23-29, 1994).

69. Ibid.

70. Ibid.

71. Ibid.

72. Ibid.

73.   Ibid.

74.   Ibid.

75.   Ibid.

76.   Ibid.

77.   Ibid.

78.   "Walk in fear," *The Economist*, 39.

79.   Lewis, "Islam and Liberal Democracy," 98.

80.   Lewis, "Islam and Liberal Democracy," 96.

81.   International Covenant on Civil and Political Rights, United Nations General Assembly Resolution 2200 (XXI), 21 U.N. GAOR, Supp. (No. 16) 52 U.N. Doc. A/6316 (1967), reprinted in 6 I.L.M. 368 (1967).

82.   Universal Declaration of Human Rights, Dec. 10, 1948, United Nations General Assembly Resolution 217 A (III), U.N. Doc. A/810, at 71 (1948).

83.   For the plight of women in traditional Muslim countries, see generally Brooks, *NINE PARTS DESIRE: The Hidden World of Islamic Women*; Mahmoody with Hoffer, *NOT WITHOUT MY DAUGHTER*; Sahebjam, *The Stoning of Soraya M.*; Sasson, *PRINCESS: A True Story Of Life Behind The Veil In Saudi Arabia*.

84.   "Islam and the West," *The Economist*, 11 (August 6-12, 1994).

85.   "'Divorce Iranian Style' In Court, Islamic Law Favors the Husband," *The Wall Street Journal*, A1, A8 (Tuesday, November 8, 1994).

86.   "Islam and the West," *The Economist*, 11.

87.   Ibid.

88. "Al Azhar joins the Vatican," *The Economist*, 34, 35 (August 27-September 2, 1994).

89. *The Cambridge Encyclopedia*, 167.

90. Ibid.

91. See generally *The Cambridge Encyclopedia*, 167-168.

92. Ibid.

93. *The Cambridge Encyclopedia*, 168.

94. "Walk in fear," *The Economist*, 39.

95. "Nothing to lose but your chador," *The Economist*, 43 (August 7-13, 1993).

96. Ibid.

97. Ibid.

98. Rushdie, "One Thousand Days in a Balloon," *The Rushdie Letters: Freedom to Speak, Freedom to Write*, 15, 24.

99. "Backlash," *The Economist*, 42 (October 22-28, 1994).

100. Ibid.

101. Ibid.

102. "Islam and the West," *The Economist*, 11-12.

103. *The Cambridge Encyclopedia*, 167.

104. "Bishop's Killing Puts Focus on Persecution in Iran," *The New York Times*, A20 (Sunday, February 6, 1994).

105. Ibid.

106. Ibid.

107. Ibid.

108. Locke, *A Letter concerning Toleration: with the Second Treatise of Civil Government*, 160.

109. His Holiness John Paul II, *Crossing The Threshold Of Hope*, 91.

110. Ibid., 93-94.

111. Ibid., 94.

112. Kepel, *MUSLIM EXTREMISM IN EGYPT: The Prophet And Pharaoh*, 204-210.

113. "Fundamentalists Impose Culture on Egypt," *The New York Times*, A1, A10 (Thursday, February 3, 1994); see also Sivan, "Eavesdropping on Radical Islam," 22-24.

114. International Covenant on Civil and Political Rights, United Nations General Assembly Resolution 2200 (XXI), 21 U.N. GAOR, Supp. (No. 16) 52, U.N. Doc. A/6316 (1967), reprinted in 6 I.L.M. 368 (1967).

115. Mayer, "Islam And The State," 1050-1052.

116. Ibid., 1051, footnote 119; *The New York Times*, A6 (March 17, 1989).

117. "Heavy guard for writer on Paris visit," *Hartford Courant*, A21 (November 24, 1994).

118. Mayer, "Islam And The State," 1047-1050.

119. Samuel P. Huntington has written about the friction points between the Christian (i.e., Western) and Muslim worlds in his article "The Clash of Civilizations." Prof. Huntington believes the two civilizations are incompatible in various respects and may be destined for conflict.

CHAPTER THREE

BIRTH OF AN EMPIRE

It's a matter of time...In 10 years you
will have quite a number of countries"
united under the banner of Islamic
fundamentalism.
-Hassan al-Turabi, leader of Sudan's
ruling Islamic Front.
-August, 1993[1].

"We have potentially big power in other
countries. In the Muslim states and
even in Europe and the U.S. our
resources are the Muslims who are
with the Islamic Revolution. Our
enemies are panicked at our power
abroad and at the presence of the
Islamic Revolution in other lands."
-Ali Akbar Mohtashemi, then head of
Iran's Defense and Islamic
Revolutionary Guard Corps Committee.
-March, 1993[2].

I. Stirrings of Muslim Consciousness

So far, this study has established that the branch of Islam popularly known
as fundamentalist has a profound hatred for all things Western and has a
history of engaging in political violence, subversion, terrorism and
assassination in order to achieve its political ends. As part of their
takeover strategy, the radical fundamentalists typically have first declared
war on their own secular governments whom they view as having "sold out"
to Western interests. Those governments, like Egypt's, that purport to
uphold Islamic values without fully and wholeheartedly instituting the
sharia or traditional Islamic law are attacked as "un-Islamic" by the

fundamentalists. The inability of many secular governments (whether they are socialist, democratic or a military-backed dictatorship) throughout North Africa and the Middle East to deliver on their economic promises makes them particularly vulnerable to political subversion. The world decline in oil prices (oil being the primary export of many of these countries) during the 1980s and 1990s has led to increased unemployment and has only further exacerbated the situation. To a largely young and uneducated populace, the fundamentalists' somewhat simplistic slogan "Islam is the solution" sounds like it is at least worth a try.

Another striking characteristic of the rise of radical Islamic movements in many countries is the broad-based nature of this revolutionary movement. Fundamentalist activity is not limited to the words and deeds of a few well-organized and well-financed terrorist cells[3].

Fundamentalist Muslims have penetrated and taken over many professional societies in Egypt including the medical societies and the legal bar. The Muslim Brotherhood has set up neighborhood medical clinics and offers other social services which give it a profile at the local level and power among the populace. These activities constitute a very successful form of grass roots political organizing.

The idea of reordering society solely along Muslim lines has also been a frequent refrain heard on radio and TV within the Muslim world. The fundamentalist world view has even been successfully injected into the curriculum of many schools. Except for a small, Westernized elite beholden to the government which often enriches it, fundamentalist Islamic parties can count among their ardent followers doctors, lawyers, academics, engineers, taxi drivers, street vendors and farmers among others. The movement is truly society-wide in scope.

But the rise of fundamentalist Islam is more than a domestic political phenomenon in various politically and economically challenged countries with large Muslim populations. Fundamentalist Islam is also an aggressive international revolutionary ideology characterized by i) a high degree of self-consciousness, coordination and planning among participants from many different nations, ii) a specialized revolutionary vocabulary (e.g, "the Great Satan," "global arrogance"), and iii) a "game plan" for regional and territorial conquest. Iran and Sudan are the only countries to date that are governed by radical Muslim regimes. Not surprisingly then, a discussion of the international activities of fundamentalist revolutionaries consists to some degree of a discussion of Iran's and Sudan's foreign policies and terrorist activities. As the oldest fundamentalist regime in the modern world, Iran is clearly the "Big Brother" to fledgling Muslim revolutionaries worldwide. Sudan has eagerly joined Iran's side in its literal and rhetorical "war" against the West. Given the still relatively modest size of their respective military forces, both nations for the moment have adopted terrorism as their offensive strategy against the West. Terrorism is the poor nation's logical weapon of choice against a militarily superior enemy: It is cheap for the practitioner, expensive for the victim and always deniable when circumstances warrant (e.g., when a "victim" state is about to retaliate with massive, punitive force).

As will be demonstrated below, in political-military affairs the fundamentalist Muslims have worked closely together across national borders and have begun to think and act as a transnational revolutionary movement. In the diplomatic arena as well, several Muslim nations have acted collectively to protest the international arms embargo against Bosnia. They have also jointly offered to send Muslim troops as peacekeepers to the region. On July 13, 1993 six Muslim countries - Iran, Tunisia, Turkey, Malaysia, Bangladesh and Pakistan, plus a Palestinian delegation, offered to provide the United Nations with 17,000 troops to protect U.N.-declared "safe havens" in Bosnia[4]. Iran has even gone further, offering tacit military support and training to Muslim forces fighting the Serbs. The situation in Bosnia in particular has served to raise the consciousness of the traditional Muslim world and remind Muslims of their distinctiveness from the Christian West. Given the lackluster performance of the United Nations and the shameful partition plan offered by Lord Owen and former Carter Administration Secretary of State Cyrus Vance, the Muslim world has become convinced that Europe cares less for Muslim lives than it does for Christian ones. The war in the former Yugoslavia has only served to stir feelings of a common cultural and religious identity among many Muslims and to deepen fundamentalist Muslim resentment of the West.

In the economic and commercial spheres, there are stirrings of a Muslim rennaisance throughout Central Asia and portions of the Middle East. Iran, Pakistan and Turkey have already established economic and diplomatic ties to the former Soviet Central Asian republics[5]. Turning their backs on their Russian conquerors of a century and more before, the Central Asian nations are forging close ties with their Muslim brothers to the south. There are plans for rail lines, roads and pipelines for transporting natural gas, oil and other materials to the south[6]. For its part, Iran earnestly hopes to greatly increase its military strength through the purchase of nuclear weapons, intermediate range missiles, long range bombers, fighters, tanks and other weaponry from the former Soviet arsenal located within the Central Asian republics. The fundamentalists' military and political initiatives in Asia and Africa are discussed more fully below.

II. The Islamintern

Soon after establishing themselves firmly in Russia, the Communists founded the Comintern, an organization created for the express purpose of exporting Communist ideals abroad and assisting Communist revolutionaries in toppling non-Communist governments in other countries[7]. Is there an organization or group we might call for lack of a better name the "Islamintern"?   Do the radical Islamic fundamentalists have a similar blueprint for toppling other governments in the region and seizing control? There are actually at least two groups that have planned, coordinated and exported fundamentalist Islamic revolution and violence to other countries. The first group is an Iranian military brigade called Qods Force, a group affiliated with the fanatical Revolutionary Guards. The second organization is a planning group sponsored by Iran and Sudan but encompassing Islamic revolutionaries from many different nations known as the Islamic Arab Popular Conference, a benign sounding title for a deadly organization.   These organizations are more than terrorist planning groups sponsored by two outlaw Muslim states.   They are dedicated to the overthrow of "infidel" and "atheist" governments in the region and to the establishment and consolidation of radical Muslim regimes in their place. These groups are truly pan-Islamic in their outlook and objectives.

A. Qods Force

The Islamic Republic of Iran has created a revolutionary military brigade called Qods Force (meaning "Jerusalem" in Farsi) specifically for the purpose of fomenting fundamentalist rebellion and violence in other nations in furtherance of radical Islam's imperialist and expansionist aims[8]. The group's founding commander is Brig. General Ahmed Vahidi. An indication of Qods Forces importance to the Iranian regime is the fact that Vahidi reports directly to President Hashemi Rafsanjani, the so-called "moderate" Iranian leader, and is answerable to no one else. The director of operations of Qods Force is Commander Mosleh. Mosleh has an extensive background in murder, terrorism and intrigue having led the infamous Revolutionary Guards in Lebanon from 1982 to 1984 and having apparently masterminded the bombing of the U.S. Marine barracks in Beirut in 1983. Qods Force director of intelligence Mohammed Jafari comes to his job with prior experience planning terrorist attacks in Europe. The agency has opened a training center in the Imam Ali Garrison, just outside of Tehran in one of the Shah's former palaces, for the purpose of training fanatical recruits from Saudi Arabia, Egypt, Algeria and the Central Asian republics in the arts of spying, political subversion, assassination and terrorism.

Qods Force agents have been active on many fronts outside Iran working to subvert legitimate governments and support Islamic fundamentalist terrorists and revolutionaries. For example, Commander Qa'ani, head of the so-called Fourth Division of Qods Force known as the Ansar Corps, has apparently been assigned the mission to undermine and overthrow the legitimate governments of the newly independent Central Asian republics with the goal of establishing fundamentalist Islamic dictatorships allied with Iran. The Ansar Corps has also reportedly actively supported the terrorist organization PKK (Kurdish Workers Party) which seeks by extreme means to break away from Turkey and establish an independent Kurdish state.

In 1992, Iran sent 10,000 soldiers to Sudan of which 2,000 were Qods Force troops. The Qods Force soldiers were sent there primarily to help the radical Sunni regime in Khartoum suppress a rebellion by the Christian population fighting for independence in the south. While in Sudan, the Qods Force operatives also worked to export fundamentalist revolutionary ideas and violence across the border to nearby Egypt and Saudi Arabia. Upper Egypt suffered a wave of violence and crime precipitated by Qods Force activities and had to be placed under the protection of 4,000 Egyptian riot police and 2,000 regular soldiers. Many Egyptian citizens of the Coptic Christian faith living in the area were the victims of assault (some attacks were unfortunately fatal), robbery and property damage caused by Islamic fundamentalists. A number of fundamentalists were apprehended and taken off the streets and into custody. During the course of these arrests, many caches of automatic weapons were discovered in Islamic fundamentalist hands in Egypt.

The Iranians have also lavishly supported fundamentalist violence in Algeria. The intelligence agencies of both France and Morocco have reported that Iran gave in excess of $100 million and possibly as much as $200 million to the Islamic Salvation Front in support of their political and revolutionary activities in Algeria.

In the east, Iran has established ties to the brutal Afghan freedom fighter Gulbuddin Hekmatyar, an Islamic fundamentalist who admires Iran's form of government. Hekmatyar's enthusiastic use and endorsement of torture and terrorism has even alienated him from his courageous, freedom fighting Afghan allies including Ahmed Shad Massoud, the freedom fighter known as "The Lion of Panshir." Iran's material and moral support for Hekmatyar through Qods Force and the Iranian Revolutionary Guards does not bode well for the political stability of the Indian subcontinent.

B. The Islamic Arab Popular Conference

In April of 1991, Islamic revolutionaries from many different countries gathered in the city of Khartoum in Sudan to craft a blueprint for the overthrow of non-Islamic regimes throughout Africa and the Middle East and to ponder and actively plan for the creation of a new world order along Islamic lines. Known as the Islamic Arab Popular Conference, the convocation was attended by every major radical Islamic party including several underground terrorist organizations[9]. The Muslim Brotherhood of Egypt, Algeria's Islamic Salvation Front, Tunisia's Islamic opposition movement known as al-Nahda, Afghanistan's Hezb-i-Islami faction (represented by the notorious rebel leader Gulbuddin Hekmatyar), senior delegates from Iran and Sudan and several leftist and nationalist revolutionary figures all attended the session.

The group issued a six point manifesto which ominously and violently lashed out at America and the West and proclaimed the righteousness of Islam. While mouthing the words of peace, tolerance and diplomacy, the international fundamentalist Islamic movement clearly demonstrated its antipathy and deep-seated hostility toward Western governments and society in its pronouncements during the conference.

The group also made an attempt to begin reuniting the two major Islamic sects. Hassan al-Turabi, the leader of Sudan's ruling National Islamic Front and the host of the conference, expressed his desire that the Sunni and Shi'a factions would unite for the greater good of worldwide Islam thereby ending the rift between the two factions that has existed since the 7th century[10].

The conference, and the picture of international coordination and cooperation between Islamic radicals and terrorists of different stripes and religious sects that it presented, represented historic first steps toward uniting the Islamic world along politico-religious lines. Although barely reported in the Western media, the significance of the conference was not lost on its participants. Mr. Turabi, an interesting and intelligent figure in his own right who also happens to be a Western-educated jurist, has boasted that Western policymakers are even more fearful of Islamic fundamentalism than they ever were of the worldwide Communist threat[11]. Turabi has worked steadily to unite the Islamic world and has publicly predicted that it is only a matter of time, perhaps 10 years, before a sizable number of countries in Africa, the Middle East and Asia are led by Islamic fundamentalist regimes which would cooperate with one another on many fronts against Western interests.

C. The Islamic World Order: A Hint of Things to Come

Islamic fundamentalism is the language of political opposition throughout North Africa, Central Asia and the Middle East today. The movement's base of support is growing steadily day by day, particularly among the young and the poor who constitute by far the two largest categories of people in the Middle East and North Africa. If Mr. Turabi's prediction about the worldwide expansion of radical Islam comes to pass, it is highly likely that an "Islamic Bloc" will emerge on the world scene which will act as a single unit diplomatically and militarily.

Whether this Islamic Bloc remains a military alliance like NATO or the Warsaw Pact, a confederation much like the old British Empire during the last century or an Islamic Empire on the order of the old Arab or Ottoman Empires is immaterial from the standpoint of Western security interests. Regardless, the West will need to develop a diplomatic and strategic "master plan" to respond to this violently hostile movement. This author believes that an actual monolothic empire exhibiting strong signs of centralized political and military control is the most likely scenario given traditional Islam's penchant for top-down leadership, the largely Islamic Third World's general lack of experience with and exposure to democracy and decentralized forms of governance and the historic willingness of Islam's adherents enthusiastically and unflinchingly to surrender their civil and political rights to a strong leader.

III. Islam: The Tie That Binds

Looking back at 1300 years of Islamic and Middle Eastern history, it is evident that whenever the Muslim world has attempted to unite politically on a grand scale it has always succeeded when it has used a native or indigenous ideology as its unifying principle, and it has always failed whenever it has used a non-indigenous philosophy as the basis of unification. Several examples illustrate this point.

A. Unification Failures

In the late 19th and early 20th century, the European concepts of nationalism and colonialism wreaked havoc on the peoples of the Middle East and Muslim world. The European powers carved up the Middle East at that time into nations which bore little or no relationship to the racial, ethnic and religious divisions that exist in that part of the world. Nationalism, as unilaterally imposed on the region by the Europeans, has only served to divide the Muslims. The bitter warfare between Iraq and Iran during the 1980s in which Muslim killed Muslim illustrates this point. The individual citizen's loyalty to the largely artificially constructed nations of Turkey, Syria, Jordan or Iraq has actually hindered not helped the cause of Islamic unity.

Later in the 20th century, Communist ideals were imported into the region from the U.S.S.R. and Eastern Europe. Many Muslim and Arab leaders in the region modelled their governments after this ideology and found that while Communism and socialism helped them plan their economies (usually badly, in retrospect) and structure their schools and institutions of government, it did not enable any one of them to unite the Muslim world under a common banner. Egyptian leader Gamal Abdel Nasser was the undisputed spokesman of the Arab world during the 1950s and early 1960s[12]. Nasser ruled Egypt through his Free Officers party, which was the name of the Arab socialist movement in Egypt. Despite his popularity, he was unable to unite the Arab world politically. He made repeated attempts to unify the Muslim Middle East but had only minimal success. In 1958, Nasser's Egypt and Baathist Syria (Syria's ruling socialist party) announced the formation of a new nation, the United Arab Republic ("UAR"). North Yemen, an old style Islamic nation, later joined the UAR which lasted officially until the early 1960s. However, the United Arab Republic was little more than a name and was plagued by tensions and political difficulties from the start. Nasser's dreams of Arab unity were stillborn. The hammer and sickle was plainly incapable of standing firmly in the sands of the Middle East and North Africa.

B. Unification Success

In contrast, the Muslim world has always met with success when it has organized its people, culture and resources along Islamic lines. Islam as the organizing principle of the state made the ancient Arab Empire great and brought centuries of prosperity and success to the Ottoman Turks as well. Islam has provided its people with more than a common religion. It has provided many different ethnic and tribal groups with a common culture, identity, world political view and, in many cases, a common language. (The Koran is written in Arabic). Now that Communism is out of vogue, it is likely that leaders of largely Muslim populations will turn back to the religion of their birth as an organizing principle. Unlike other ideologies, Islam is indigenous to the Middle East and North Africa and has a centuries long history outside these areas as well due to past conquests by the Arabs and Ottoman Turks. The signs are auspicious for future political unification within the vast Islamic world along explicitly Islamic lines.

Much has been said about nationalism's renewed power in the late 20th century to destroy polyglot empires like the Soviet Union and multi-ethnic nations like Yugoslavia. Some may wonder whether such centrifugal forces will undermine the potential for unity within the Islamic world as well. It is the author's heartfelt opinion that the revival of nationalist feeling, which is itself an expression of renewed ethnic and religious identity, will help not hurt the process of unification within the Islamic world. Islam is a common cultural and religious denominator for millions of people across Asia, Africa and the Middle East. The stirring of ethnic and religious feeling and the search for communal identity after the collapse of Communism has increased many people's awareness of their common Islamic roots. Thus, the resurgent role of ethnic and religious identity in state politics, often characterized as a form of nationalism, ultimately will aid Islam's establishment as a political force across wide areas of the globe.

Prof. Ernest Gellner has taken a somewhat different approach in answering the question of the interplay between Islam and nationalism. However, his conclusion is the same as the author's. Islam is a powerful identifying and unifying force among Muslim peoples.

> Islam can perform precisely the function which nationalism has performed elsewhere; provide a new self-image for people no longer able to identify with their position in village, lineage, clan or tribe[13].

Gellner perceives Islam as a substitute for nationalism in those areas where Islam dominates. In contrast, the author would argue that the search for communal identity that nationalist feelings unleash will ultimately lead the peoples of the Middle East, Central Asia and North Africa to a fundamentalist form of Islam as the foundation of their state and society. In this sense, Islam might be viewed as an outgrowth of or as the ultimate expression of essentially "nationalist" feelings. Indeed, one commentator recently went so far as to call Islamic fundamentalism "a form of 'national' resistance," to the West and other outside, i.e., non-Muslim or not authentically Muslim, forces[14].

Nationalist feelings have led to the formation of an Orthodox Greater Serbia on the ashes of the former Yugoslavia, an expansive, muscle-flexing Armenia, and the founding of a fledgling Chechen state inside the former Soviet Union, among others. Serbia and Armenia, in particular, have looked to their distant past as a source of guidance, inspiration and psychological support. The ancient kingdom of Armenia last flourished during the time of the Roman Empire. It is primarily knowledge of the boundaries of that ancient kingdom which has prompted modern day Armenia to look longingly and sometimes hungrily upon its neighbors. Similarly, the Serbs seem obsessed by their medieval defeats at the hands of the Ottoman Turks and are determined to regain all of their former territory.

If Armenians and Serbs have been prompted by nationalism to look to their own past for guidance and in ordering their domestic and foreign policies, then Muslims may be similarly influenced to do the same. The territorial scope of the Arab and Ottoman Empires still mirrors the location of Muslim populations today. The memories of past greatness and territorial acquisition may indeed furnish the basis for founding a modern Islamic super-state. Given the resurgence of Islam in political life generally and the increasing friction between the more radical parts of the Islamic world and the Judeo-Christian West, it would not be at all surprising to witness the appearance of a modern Islamic Empire, born out of the power vacuum created by the end of the Cold War and the disintegration of the Soviet Empire. A nation or empire founded upon a religious ideal (fundamentalist Islam) should seem no more far-fetched, at least in the realm of ideas, than nations founded upon abstract political ideals (e.g., liberal democracy, Marxist-Leninism).

IV. The Rising Tide: A Survey of Militant Islamic Movements in Several Key Nations

How is radical Islam currently doing in its attempt to seize power? Islamic regimes are, of course, already firmly in place in Sudan and Iran, the two linchpins of the radical Islamic revolution. These nations have been working steadily to export their brand of religious dictatorship to other regions of the world. In particular, Iran has made steady inroads within the newly independent Central Asian republics[15]. These new Asian nations have predominantly Muslim populations, and share a common culture and a common language with their fellow believers in Iran and Turkey. Like the Iranians, citizens of Tajikistan speak Farsi while the other republics speak a Turkic dialect[16]. As we saw in an earlier segment of this work, these republics possess advanced weaponry including (in the case of Kazakhstan) nuclear weapons, long range bombers, intercontinental missiles and significant amounts of conventional Soviet military equipment. Iran is eager to get its hands on this war material. In fact, there is some evidence that one or more of these Muslim nations has already sold advanced weaponry to Iran.

The nations of Azerbaijan, Turkmenistan, Uzbekistan, Tajikistan, Kazakhstan and Kyrgyzstan all have flourishing Islamic political movements eager to assume power[17]. The Islamic Renaissance Party is active in all of the Central Asian states and has already shown itself to be a potent political force. In 1991, four of these nations banned all activities of this party out of fear of its growing strength. In addition to the Islamic Renaissance Party, the Islamic activists can be found under several different banners ranging from the Alush in Kazakhstan to more obscure cells of followers organized around local mosques and particular religious leaders.

Islam has played an ancient and longstanding role in the political life of Central Asia. Arriving in the eighth century, the religion achieved prominence in Asia during the medieval reigns of Genghis Khan and Tamerlane[18]. Islam has been a part of tribal and nomadic life ever since. The resilience of the religion and the firm grip it exerted on adherents over the centuries was demonstrated in the 1920s. By that time, czarist Russia and later the Soviet Union had long since conquered the region and driven Islamic cultural and religious folkways underground through the imposition of Russian as the official language, the cyrillic alphabet, a system of territorial partition designed to break the back of potential religious and ethnic-based opposition to the conquerers from Moscow and through other means. Nonetheless, during the Russian civil war of 1918-1921 Basmachi rebels declared an independent Muslim state known as the Turkestan Independent Islamic Republic. While the fledgling nation was quickly conquered by the Reds, its brief existence indicated that Islam was still a potent organizing force for those living in the region.

As in other parts of the world, fundamentalist Islam has become the language of political opposition in Central Asia. Cut loose from Moscow, the old Communist elites still in power in many Asian republics are being challenged not by secular democratic movements but by Islamic ones. It is important to bear in mind that unlike the teachings of Islam, democracy is an alien concept to the millions of people who live in Central Asia. Some experts have predicted that it would probably take a generation for the population in that region of the world to become accustomed to the workings of democracy and the free enterprise system[19]. In the current political contest between Islam and democracy, Islam is already winning hands down.

The Islamic Republic of Iran has welcomed and encouraged this religious and political revival of Islam. In the fall of 1991, Iran's foreign minister Ali Akbar Velayati was the first foreign minister to visit these new nations. Since then, Iran has sought to play a significant role in the internal affairs of these states ranging from playing regional peace broker when such services have been needed (for example in mediating the Azeri-Armenian dispute over Nagorno-Karabakh) to providing technical and economic assistance. Iran's diplomatic, intelligence and military services now have offices and a foothold in these republics.

The prospect of strengthening economic ties will only further cement the relationships already being forged by the common religious and cultural identity which Iran and these nations share with one another. Given Iran's common borders with the region and its ability to offer the Central Asian nations access to the sea via an overland route to the port of Bandar Abbas, Iran is clearly the front runner in the worldwide contest to establish deep and enduring commercial relationships with these nations. In fact, an Islamic economic cooperation council of sorts along the lines of the more well known European Economic Community already exists. Iran, Turkey and Pakistan expanded their Economic Cooperation Organization in February, 1992 to include every Muslim republic in Central Asia except Kazakhstan, which declined for the moment to join out of sensitivity to its significant Russian minority[20].

Further west, at the bridge between Asia and Europe, the story is much the same. The officially secular government of Turkey finds itself increasingly challenged at the polls by Islamic revivalists who wish to abolish Western influences and reshape the nation and Turkish society along fundamentalist Islamic lines[21]. A member of the fundamentalist Islamic Welfare (Refah) Party recently won the mayoral race in Turkey's largest city Istanbul. Turkey's capitol Ankara also recently fell under the control of the Welfare Party[22].

Turkey's secular identity springs from the ashes of the Ottoman Empire. After the fall of that regime at the end of World War I, Turkey under the leadership of the reformer and political leader Kemal Attaturk instituted an essentially European system of representative government and pushed Islam back into the mosque where many thought it belonged[23]. Since then, Turkey has uneasily straddled the two continents and two cultures of Muslim Asia and Christian (e.g., politically secular) Europe. Having watched the killing of Muslims in Bosnia-Herzegovina by Christian Serbs and the killing of Muslim Azeris by Christian Armenians in the disputed region of Nagorno-Karabakh located in Azerbaijan, Turkish sympathies are now being pulled strongly in the direction of Islam. Inflation, increased foreign debt and declining productivity have also fanned the flames of Islamic extremism by hurting Turkish living standards and undermining the popularity of Turkey's secular, pro-Western government[24].

Experts at grass-roots organization and mass recruiting techniques, the fundamentalists have built a formidable political machine. According to recent public opinion polls, the Welfare Party is in first place, ahead of the two centrist parties - the Motherland Party and former Prime Minister Tansu Ciller's True Path Party. Approximately two thirds of Turkey's 60 million citizens now live in towns or districts controlled by Welfare Party officials. The Party's ranks have been swelled in recent years by displaced Kurds, millions of whom have fled their homes in the countryside due to the ongoing insurgency there and have settled in the poorest sections of Turkey's major cities. Frequently unable to find gainful employment and accustomed to more conservative social mores than those found in the cities, the Kurds are easy marks for fundamentalist recruiters who play upon their frustration and discontent.

But the fundamentalist Islamic movement in Turkey has not waited for its increased popularity to bring it eventual victory through the polls. For the past few years, in the manner of all terrorists, murderers and thugs, Islamic activists have sought to bomb, intimidate and assassinate their way into power. Turkish politicians advocating a continued secular course for that nation's form of government have not been debated. Instead, they have been systematically targeted for death. In 1990, for example, 21 prominent political figures were murdered by the Islamic movement in the Turkish cities of Istanbul, Ankara and Bursa.

In the case of Turkey, as with the other Muslim nations discussed herein, there is very little need to speculate about the political designs of its religious leaders. Islamic activists repeatedly have voiced their dark and violent vision of the future in countless slogans, platforms and speeches. The Welfare Party has worked to close battered women's shelters and segregate buses by sex[25]. It has also attacked ballet as a degenerate art form. This political party has even attempted to destroy historical monuments and relics which do not portray the nation's Muslim past.

Party leaders advocated tearing down Istanbul's ancient fortress walls because they were remnants of the city's Byzantine past. Only an outcry among members of the public prevented the proposal from going forward. In addition to a program of social revolution and cultural destruction the Muslim fundamentalists envision unity with other fundamentalist Muslims and fundamentalist nations like Iran. After recent successes in Turkey's municipal elections, Welfare Party leader Mecmettin Erbakan promised that his party would "save Turkey ... save Islamic unity" and "save humanity."[26] Erbakan, like his fundamentalist brethren, dreams of founding a religious utopia not just in his native country but among all like minded Muslims across wide areas of the globe. His messianic pledge to "save humanity" is perhaps the most ominous of the three statements since it implies that the fundamentalist Muslims might be bringing their own brand of "salvation" to the rest of the world.

Even Turkey's secular leadership seems drawn to the worldly possibilities inherent in a revitalized Islamic super-state. Ominously, the late Turkish President Turgut Ozal referred in an interview with the German magazine *Der Spiegel* on December 23, 1991 to a new Islamic-Turkic empire, "a Greater Turkey," along the lines of the old Ottoman Empire. In that interview, he stated in part that "[c]urrent historical circumstances permit Turkey to reverse the shrinking process that began at the walls of Vienna."[27] He was referring to the Ottoman seige of Vienna in 1683. Incredibly, Turkey's Kemalist secular government already seems to be looking toward its successor - a future Islamic empire founded in the Middle East and Central Asia. Whether Turkey's ambitions can be squared with Iran's remains to be seen. This author predicts however, that Turkey under the Islamic fundamentalists will have everything in common with their Iranian co-religionists.

Afghanistan has been bathed in the blood of Islamic revolutionary violence since the pullout of the Soviet Army in the last 1980s. Kabul and other cities have suffered more damage as the result of fundamentalists than they suffered during the war with the Soviet Union. When and if that tortured country ever emerges from its death spiral a radical Islamic fundamentalist regime will likely be at the helm[28]. Recently, a little known fundamentalist force called the Taliban has succeeded in pushing competing militias out of Kabul and appears poised to overthrow the Rabbani Government. Flushed with success, the Taliban has refused to enter into U.N. mediated negotiations with the government. In areas where the group has already established control, the Taliban has strictly enforced the most rigorous of Islamic norms. The citizens of Kabul fear the coming fundamentalist rule of this latest group of Muslim purists.

Radical Islam continues to make steady inroads in each of the North African nations. Some of these movements have been addressed previously. The Muslim Brotherhood and other militant groups in Egypt continue their campaign of assassination, violence and terrorism against members of the government, Egyptian citizens and foreign visitors. The radical Muslim group Jamaat al-Jihad was responsible for the murder of President Anwar Sadat in October, 1981 and is also responsible for many of the recent attacks on Western tourists in that country. The Egyptian tourist industry has been decimated by Islamic terrorism and the campaign of political assassinations continues unabated. Egypt's top anti-terrorist minister, Maj. Gen. Raouf Khayrat, was assassinated by Muslim militants outside his home on April 9, 1994[29].

The Islamic militants have the greatest hope of near term success in Algeria where the military-backed secular government looks shakier every day. The respected British newsmagazine *The Economist* has called the collapse of Algeria "highly probable" and has predicted "its replacement by a singularly intransigent bunch of Islamic rebels, fundamentalists of the most bloody-minded sort."[30] The Islamic Salvation Front is already a formidable political force. Had national elections not been cancelled in December, 1991, it is very likely that this Islamic group would have captured a plurality in the parliament. Since being forced underground the Islamic Salvation Front and its ally the Armed Islamic Movement have turned to murdering prominent intellectuals and secularists. For example, on August 21, 1993, former Algerian prime minister Kasdi Merbah, age 55, was killed along with his son, brother, bodyguard and chauffeur[31]. Mr. Merbah opposed the imposition of Islamic law and system of government upon the people of Algeria. A large part of the Algerian army, particularly junior officers and the enlisted ranks, are suspected of sympathizing with the Islamic militants. If a full-scale civil war should erupt, it is probable that some or a large part of the Algerian military would abandon the government and side with the rebels[32]. A radical Islamic victory in Algeria, an outcome that is looking more likely every day, would give strength and hope to Islamic militants everywhere. Morocco, Tunisia and

Egypt would be the likely next victims of an Islamic terror campaign following any eventual victory in Algeria. Both Tunisia and Morocco have relatively sluggish economies and shaky leadership. In Morocco, sixty-five year old King Hassan has yet to hand the reigns of power over to the crown prince[33]. As a result, the crown prince has no experience ruling a nation at a time when Morocco is facing increasing challenges from the radical Muslims.

Radical Islamic movements and highly secretive Islamic terrorist cells are alive and well across North Africa and the Middle East from Tunisia and Morocco to Libya and Syria. Indeed, Libya's Khadaffi and Syria's Assad, two old style Communist dictators, sit on a tinderbox of growing Islamic discontent within their own countries. Only by becoming more overtly "Islamic" in manners, sympathies, rhetoric and dress have Assad and Khadaffi been able to remain in power and profit from the upsurge in fundamentalist feeling. Assad crushed the Muslim Brotherhood in 1982, killing several thousand members and their families and imprisoning others. Nonetheless, there is widespread speculation inside Syria that radical Islam will once again become a force inside the country[34].

Jordan also has a flourishing Islamic movement that has come out into the open with the institution of more democratic reforms[35]. Jordan's heavily Palestinian population means that domestic politics are largely a reflection of Palestinian attitudes toward the PLO-Israeli peace accord and the primary sponsor of that accord, the United States. Jordan's population was stridently anti-Western during the 1991 Persian Gulf War and historically has enthusiastically supported groups like the Islamic Resistance Movement, otherwise known as HAMAS[36]. HAMAS has steadfastly opposed the peace process and has attempted to disrupt good relations between Israel and the Palestinian people through murder and acts of terrorism.

Lebanon has become another casualty of the march of fundamentalist Islam. The terrorist group Hezbollah (Party of God) seeks to establish a fundamentalist state in Lebanon along the lines of the Islamic Republic of Iran and receives substantial funding, training and support from the Iranian Government[37].

The Persian Gulf dynasties face their own problems with Islamic radicals. During the Gulf War, many individuals in those states grumbled about "atheist" Western troops on their soil and the fact that they had effectively allied themselves with "the Jewish enemy." Saudi Arabia was confronted at the time with a statement signed by 107 prominent religious leaders in that country which made these very criticisms and also complained more generally about Western influences in Saudi life such as American television programs that "glorify decadent Western life-styles."[38] In the past, the oil dynasties of the Persian Gulf essentially "bought" their citizens' political complacency and acquiescence through the distribution of oil revenue. But the distribution of oil revenue can only go so far in placating the populace and stemming the rising tide of Islamic fundamentalism. As crude oil prices have declined during the 1980s and early 1990s so has the revenue realized by its sale. The Faustian bargain no longer looks so enticing to the populace, and some are now demanding a greater role in government.

The ruling Saudi dynasty currently faces an increasingly vocal and hostile Islamic opposition[39]. These radical Muslims criticize the regime for its Western ties. At times their opposition to U.S.-Saudi ties has grown violent. On November 13, 1995 five American military advisors were killed in a car bombing at a Riyadh National Guard base[40]. For its part, the Saudi regime, like Egypt's, suspects that revolutionary Iran and perhaps Sudan are behind Islamic agitation in the country. At the same time, the United States and other Western nations are pressing these countries to open up their governmental systems and hold national democratic elections. Oman, the United Arab Emirates, Qatar, Bahrain, Saudi Arabia and Kuwait are all facing internal and external pressure to open their governments to broader participation at a time when it is increasingly likely that fundamentalist Islamic forces would win any electoral contest for control.

The situation in Saudi Arabia has recently grown more complex as Washington's steadfast ally King Fahd has turned over power to his half brother and designated successor Crown Prince Abdullah ibn Abdulaziz[41]. This development may not bode well for the West. The Crown Prince opposed the stationing of U.S. troops in Saudi Arabia during the Gulf War and has opposed further Westernization and secularization of Saudi society in favor of closer ties to other traditional Arab states[42]. Thought to be weaker than his half brother King Faud, the transition of power to the Crown Prince may eventually lead Saudi Arabia closer to the fundamental ists' camp, either through more cordial relations with Iran and Sudan or greater concessions to fundamentalists at home or both.

Yemen has been a sanctuary and staging area for Islamic fundamentalists for some time[43]. The Yemeni press often reported during the 1980s that the country was being used as a jumping off point for radical mujahideen fighters on their way to fight the Soviets in Afghanistan. More recently, the terrorist group Islamic Jihad has made Yemen its home on the Arabian peninsula. In December, 1992, the Muslim terrorist group bombed two hotels in the city of Aden where 100 American military personnel had been stationed as part of the United Nation's mission to Somalia. Fortunately, the American soldiers had departed by the time the bombs exploded. However, three people still lost their lives in the blasts. The Yemen government, Marxist in orientation, is another target of the Muslim fundamentalists in the country. Several have been brought to trial for assassination of government officials and other acts of terrorism. Egypt has expressed grave concern over the fact that Yemen is being used by Islamic Jihad members who have also carried out attacks against the Egyptian government as well. Faced with an active and evidently well-armed Islamic movement inside the country, Yemen eventually may succumb to the radical Muslims as well.

Militant Islamic movements now exist in Africa, Asia, the Middle East and in places as far away as Indonesia. These movements share a common vision of government and society and, in many cases a common culture and language. If current trends continue, the world will see a fundamentalist Islamic Bloc of countries that may very well unite under common leadership.

V. Building Blocks and Stepping Stones

The international fundamentalist Islamic revolution must overcome several challenges if it is to realize success on a regional or hemispheric scale. First, the revolution must put aside or otherwise resolve petty territorial, tribal and ethnic disputes and conflicts. Iran and Turkey face this obstacle. They are both Muslim states but represent somewhat different cultural traditions. Turkey hopes to successfully compete for influence in Central Asia by virtue of the common Turkic language and culture it shares with inhabitants of the Central Asian region. Turkey is also a Sunni nation as are many of these republics. Iran, for its part, has established links with its fellow Farsi-speaking brethren in Tajikistan. Iran also has a long history of contacts with the region. Iran and Turkey have come into conflict more directly over the Kurdish question. Iran has been rumoured to support Kurdistan rebels (the PPK) operating illegally inside Turkey. If the Islamic world is to achieve unification, Iran and Turkey must put aside their imperialist rivalry. This can be achieved by several events. First, it should not take the two nations long to realize that they have a common interest in suppressing Kurdish desires for an independent state. A Kurdish state or autonomous region would detract from the territory of Iran, Turkey as well as Iraq. Iran's support for the Kurdish rebels appears to be nothing more than a harrying gesture against the currently secular government of Turkey. Second, if Turkey falls to the radical Muslims, then all or virtually all political and diplomatic differences between the two countries should evaporate. Iran should have no significant international disagreements with a like-minded Islamic regime in Turkey. Provided the Muslim Refah Party wins control of Turkey (and perhaps moves the capitol back to the Ottoman city of Istanbul away from Attaturk's Ankara), Iran and Turkey should be able to work closely together in Central Asia and elsewhere. Thus, the Turko-Iranian rivalry in Central Asia would be rapidly replaced by cooperation once Iran's co-religionists take control in Ankara.

Another important stepping stone toward political unification of the Muslim world will be the healing of the breach between the Sunni and Shia branches of the Muslim religion. Sudan's Turabi has already called for Muslims to heal this theological rift. If the cooperation between Shiite Iran and the Sunni Sudanese regime is any indication of future prospects, it appears that even if the Sunnis and Shiites do not mend their theological fences the two sects are certainly capable of working smoothly and effectively with one another in the commercial, political, military and diplomatic spheres. Iran and Sudan are close allies who have cooperated on many different levels with one another. The Iranian-Sudanese relationship bodes well for future alliances between Sunni and Shia regimes worldwide. Iran has also worked closely with other radical Sunni revolutionary groups including Hamas (the Palestinian Resistance Movement), the Islamic Group of Egypt, Jihad for the Liberation of Palestine and other Sunni radicals in Algeria, Tunisia and Jordan[44]. So, the Sunni-Shia split should not prevent political cooperation and eventual unification.

The issue of communication and language within the vast Muslim world should not present a significant obstacle to consolidation of a Muslim Bloc or a unified Islamic empire. Arabic is spoken in the Middle East and North Africa itself. Regardless of living location, most Muslims in Asia, Africa and south central Europe have some knowledge of Arabic since the Koran is written in that language. In addition to Arabic, the rest of the Muslim world generally speaks either some form of Turkic dialect or Farsi, the language commonly encountered inside Iran. Some relatively small portion of the world Muslim populace speaks either Chinese, Russian or Malay but again, many of these speakers are also bilingual with some knowledge of one of the other languages mentioned above. Language should not prove to be a significant barrier to political unification. It should be remembered that Germany and Italy were able to work closely with one another immediately prior to and during World War II despite the language difference. While they were on less intimate terms with either the Germans or Italians during the 1930s and 1940s, the Japanese also formed a durable and effective diplomatic and military alliance with both nations as one of three Axis powers. So, even assuming some differences in language these differences have not proven to be a stumbling block to political and military cooperation among peoples in the past.

These are just the major stumbling blocks that must be overcome. Added to these are a multiplicity of small regional and tribal grudges and conflicts found in various regions and villages throughout the vast Muslim world. How can these be overcome? We must look to the Prophet Mohammed and the first generation of Muslims for answers.

> Even the secular historian ... must regard Islam as the decisive factor in the expansion of the Arabs. That bedouin tribes, which constantly for centuries had engaged in warfare with each other and were known to prize their independence, should have suddenly placed themselves obediently under the order of Muslim commanders is inconceivable apart from Islam. It was Islam that provided the necessary rallying cry and instilled in the bedouin warriors a sense that they were fighting in a grand cause. Whatever may have been the original material motives of the bedouin ... [they were] caught up in a movement greater than anything they had dreamt of, a movement not of their own making, which they could explain only in terms of a divine intervention in human affairs[45].

The fundamentalist Muslims appear to have a strategic "blueprint" for obtaining control in the region and even the hemisphere. The Islamic revolution appears to have outflanked Egypt and Saudi Arabia by establishing itself in Sudan. Using Sudan as a terrorist and military base for staging operations and providing training to Muslim militants from throughout the world, Muslim cadres from Iran and elsewhere have infiltrated Egypt, Algeria and even the Arabian peninsula. The probable fall of Algeria will constitute an important victory in the worldwide march of radical Islam. The takeover of Algeria will give the radical Muslims another safe haven and base of operations from which to attack and foment rebellion in Egypt, Tunisia and Morocco. Egypt, a cultural, political and religious center for the Arab and Muslim worlds (in addition to the holy shrine of Mecca in Saudi Arabia), will be the next great prize. Having surrounded that nation with hostile fundamentalist regimes, Islamic revolutionaries will be able to step up their terrorist campaign against the secular Egyptian government. Egypt may not be able to withstand such a sustained and intense onslaught.

Central Asia should also eventually fall under the spell of the Muslims given the region's historic ties to Iran and Turkey, the depth of religious influence and feeling in the region despite seventy years of Communist rule and a century or more of czarist influence, and given the Central Asian nations' collective desire to establish ties with the Muslim nations bordering their southern frontier in preference to maintaining commercial ties with their former masters in Moscow.

Having consolidated their rule in Central Asia, the Middle East and North Africa, the radical Muslims will then be free to give full expression to their hatred of the West. The capture of Egypt, Saudi Arabia and the formerly Soviet Central Asian republics will give the Islamic Empire a tremendous military and nuclear arsenal as well as impressive natural resources, which is the subject of the next chapter. With these resources, the Islamic Empire will not need to depend on the West. It will be free to increase its literal and rhetorical war against America and Europe without fear of a punishing, Gulf War-style military campaign since its robust military forces and sizable nuclear arsenal will prevent a quick and painless victory by Western forces. Indeed, its nuclear arsenal and other weapons of mass destruction may prevent any form of military retaliation at all by the West. By the dawn of the twenty-first century, the West will face a new, hostile and increasingly aggressive imperialist power on the world stage.

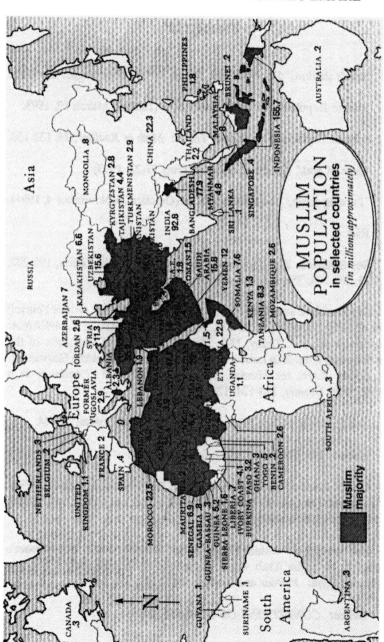

MUSLIM POPULATION
in selected countries
(in millions, approximately)

Muslim majority

ENDNOTES

1.   "Iran's shadow," *The New York Times*, E1 (Sunday, August 22, 1993).

2.   Islamic Republic of Iran News Agency (IRNA), March 19, 1993.

3.   John L. Esposito, *The Islamic Threat: Myth or Reality?*, 23, 132-133.

4.   "Fear of god," *The Economist*, 49 (July 17-23, 1993).

5.   "Turning south," *The Economist*, 40 (October 29-November 4, 1994).

6.   Ibid.

7.   See Schapiro, *The Communist Party Of The Soviet Union*, 198-200, 222-223, 302-304, 356-358.

8.   See Davidson and Rees-Mogg, *The Great Reckoning: Protect Yourself in the Coming Depression*, 222-224, 242; Bodansky, *TARGET AMERICA: Terrorism in the U.S. Today*, 117. For a description of Iran's use of the Revolutionary Guards in Lebanon in the hope of establishing a fundamentalist regime there, see Hunter, *Iran And The World: Continuity in a Revolutionary Decade*, 123-124, 126.

9.   See generally Miller, "The Challenge of Radical Islam," 43-44.

10.   Miller, "The Challenge of Radical Islam," 44.

11.   "Iran's shadow," *The New York Times*, E1 (Sunday, August 22, 1993). For more information about Turabi and his political beliefs, see Miller, "Faces of Fundamentalism," 123.

12.   For conditions within Egypt under Gamal Nasser and Nasser's attempt to unify the Arab world in the late 1950s and early 1960s, see Hopwood, *Egypt: Politics and Society 1945-1981*, 34-104.

13.   Gellner, *CONDITIONS OF LIBERTY*, 24.

14.   Pfaff, *THE WRATH OF NATIONS*, 128.

15.   See Pipes and Clawson, "Ambitious Iran, Troubled Neighbors."

16.   Ibid., 139; Wright, "Islam and Democracy," 141.

17.   Wright, "Islam and Democracy," 140-143.

18.   Wright, "Islam and Democracy," 139.

19.   Wright, "Islam and Democracy," 140.

20.   Olcott, "Central Asia's Catapult to Independence," 108, 118.

21.   See Kuniholm, "Turkey and the West," 34; Pipes and Clawson, "Ambitious Iran, Troubled Neighbors," 134-137.

22.   "Turkey eyes Islam," *The Economist*, 46 (April 2-8, 1994); see also "The lady and the lira," *The Economist*, 52 (February 5-11, 1994); "Turning Eastward: Islamic Party's Gains In Istanbul Stir Fears of a Radical Turkey," *The Wall Street Journal*, A1 (Monday, September 11, 1994).

23.   See generally Lewis, *The Emergence of Modern Turkey*; Shaw & Ezel Kural Shaw, *History of the Ottoman Empire and Modern Turkey, Volume II: Reform, Revolution and Republic: The Rise of Modern Turkey 1808-1975.*

24.   "Discontent Seethes in Once-Stable Turkey," *New York Times*, A1, A8 (Thursday, March 2, 1995).

25.   Ibid.

26.   Ibid.

27.   *Der Spiegel*, December 23, 1991 as quoted in Pipes and Clawson, "Ambitious Iran, Troubled Neighbors," 136-137.

28.   "With Kabul largely in Ruins, Afghans Get Respite From War," *The New York Times*, A1, A7 (Monday, February 20, 1995); "New Afghan

Force Takes Hold, Turning to Peace," *The New York Times*, A3 (Thursday, February 16, 1995).

29.   "Egypt's top anti-terrorism officer slain," *The Hartford Courant*, A12 (Sunday, April 10, 1994).

30.   "Islam And The West," *The Economist*, 5-6 (August 6-12, 1994).

31.   "Shooting or voting for Islam," *The Economist*, 39 (August 28-September 2, 1994).

32.   "Islamic Rebels Gain in Fight Against Army Rule in Algeria," *The New York Times*, A2, A6 (Monday, January 24, 1994); see also "Algeria Is Edging Toward Breakup," *The New York Times*, A2, A7 (Monday, April 4, 1994).

33.   Islam And The West," *The Economist*, 7 (August 6-12, 1994).

34.   "After Assad," *The Economist*, 44 (January 22-28, 1994).

35.   Marr, "The United States, Europe, And The Middle East: An Uneasy Triangle," 211, 222.

36.   Ibid.

37.   Esposito, *The Islamic Threat: Myth Or Reality?*, 149.

38.   Pipes and Clawson, "Ambitious Iran, Troubled Neighbors," 133.

39.   "Challenge to the House of Saud," *The Economist*, 41 (October 8-14, 1994).

40.   "Crossroads at Riyadh," *The Wall Street Journal*, A14 (January 9, 1996); "Riyadh's bomb," *The Economist*, 17 (November 18-24, 1995).

41. "Crossroads in Riyadh," *The Wall Street Journal*, A14 (January 9, 1996).

42. Ibid.

43.   "A safe house?", *The Economist*, 46 (January 8-14, 1994).

44.   Phillips, "Saddamization Of Iran," 7.

45.   Weiss and Arnold H. Green, *A Survey of Arab History*, 59.

CHAPTER FOUR

RESOURCES OF THE ISLAMIC EMPIRE
AND THE POSSIBILITY OF NUCLEAR JIHAD

"There is fury, fury everywhere...Islam
is escalating and cannot be resisted.
I pray that Allah may tear apart America
just as the Soviet Union was torn apart..."
-Sheik al-Tamimi, leader of Iranian terrorist
group Islamic Jihad.
-March, 1993[1].

"It is necessary to target all U.S. objectives
throughout the world...Iranians are ready for
sacrifice and Holy War."
-Ali Akbar Mohtashemi, Iranian government
official.
-October, 1991[2].

The economic, scientific, technological, military and natural resources of
a future Islamic Empire will be considerable. First and foremost, such an
empire would be completely energy self-sufficient. For the first time in
history, the substantial oil resources of the Middle East and the vast oil
reserves of the former Soviet Central Asian republics (in particular
Azerbaijan and Kazakhstan) would be controlled by the same political
power bloc. Oil is still the lifeblood which drives the economies of the
West as well as the engines of war. Transportation, power generation and
countless industrial and manufacturing processes depend upon the use of
oil and other petroleum products. Oil is literally the foundation upon
which the highly industrialized West depends[3]. Oil is also the lifeblood of
the U.S. military and its NATO allies. Without fuel, the West would not
be able to defend itself for very long even if the U.S. was able to protect
its strategic petroleum reserves from destruction by the enemy.

With the rebound in the international economy, oil consumption in the
West is expected to rise during the rest of the century[4]. A recent United

Nations study indicates that oil output in the Russian Federation and United States continues to decline making "most of the world ... increasingly dependent on OPEC [the Organization of Petroleum Exporting Countries] for additional supplies."[5] The study goes on to state that OPEC "possesses over three quarters of the world's proved reserves of one million barrels[6]. Two thirds of these reserves are in the Persian Gulf countries..."[7] Adding the formidable oil fields of Central Asia to these figures would give any future Islamic bloc a virtual monopoly over the world's current energy supply.

The formidable position that the Islamists' would be in relative to the world's oil supply is illustrated by some other figures from the above mentioned United Nations study. The U.N. has reported that "[i]f the countries of the Persian Gulf were to produce at the current rate without ever discovering additional oil, their present reserves would last for 100 years."[8] In contrast, oil reserves in the rest of the world put together would only "last for 18 years."[9]

In sole possession of virtually all of the world's oil supplies, the Islamic powers will literally be able to hold the Western world hostage. The West has faced an oil crisis before. Dealing with OPEC, the cartel of oil exporting nations, during the 1970s was a difficult period for the West[10]. The Arab oil ministers realized that the West was absolutely dependent upon oil, and they therefore made America, Western Europe and Japan pay top dollar for that commodity. As a result, the national economies of the West went down the drain and largely stayed there for a number of years. Western citizens suffered through recession, unemployment and record breaking levels of inflation that have never been surpassed since. Meanwhile, Western governments fretted about preserving their strategic petroleum supply and worried about maintaining their military readiness at a time of acute fuel shortages.

OPEC was, however, merely a collection of savvy Arab businessmen who, after all was said and done, were willing to sell their precious commodity for the right price. The militant Islamists who may very well come to power in that strategically important area of the world share no such world view. They are not merely "capitalists with an Arab accent." Rather, they are fundamentally hostile to Western interests and values (including capitalism) and harbor nothing but ill will toward its citizens. Provided their own energy and economic needs are met through internal barter and trade, it is quite possible that the Islamic Empire that may eventually come into being will refuse absolutely to meet the West's dire need for oil. In fact, given its longstanding war with the West, it is likely that "turning off the oil faucet" will be one of the Islamic fundamentalists' *first* acts of state once they have liquidated their opposition and consolidated power internally. The energy crisis of the 1970s is going to look like a minor inconvenience in comparison to the next oil crisis of the late 20th or early 21st century.

Natural gas is another common source of fuel. Gas provides just over half of the energy supplied by oil. Oil accounted for 40.1 % of all commercial energy consumption in 1992 while gas accounted for 27.8 % of such consumption[11]. Coal, nuclear energy and hydroelectric energy supply the world's remaining energy needs. Because of the expense and difficulties associated with transporting natural gas from the site of extraction to the site of consumption, this particular fuel has not been as widely used as oil[12]. Nonetheless, the Muslim world has a stranglehold on this source of energy as well. Turkmenistan and Algeria both have sizable natural gas reserves. Algeria is the primary seller of natural gas to Europe and the largest single producer of that commodity[13]. The country accounts for approximately 70 % of Africa's entire output[14]. Other major producers include Iran, Saudi Arabia and Indonesia[15]. In terms of the location of natural gas reserves, Iran, Qatar and the United Arab Emirates account for a sizable portion of all existing reserves[16]. Iran is believed to have the second largest gas reserves in the world[17].

The Islamic Empire's other material resources also will be formidable. Covering a variety of geographic and geologic zones ranging from mountainous regions rich in minerals, areas of vast oil reserves, to plains suitable for agriculture (e.g., wheat, cotton) and the raising of livestock, the Islamic world already possesses the means to form its own virtually self-sustaining trading bloc. Residents throughout this region, from Asia and the Middle East to Africa, are accustomed to the barter system of trade. Nations as well as people living in this area have engaged in barter rather than currency payments in transacting business with one another. For example, Iran has promised Sudan oil in return for Sudan's agreement allowing the Islamic Republic to set up terrorist training camps inside Sudan and to use the country as a staging area for carrying out illegal activities in Egypt[18].

The more primitive economies found in Central Asia also have a long tradition of barter going back centuries. In fact, even under the Soviets the Central Asian republics operated partly under a commercial barter system wherein they would ship raw materials to Moscow in return for finished goods. Therefore, continued trade with the West is not a necessity for the Muslim world. Other alternative trade arrangements have been used in the recent past and can be utilized by the Muslim world again.

Alternatively, the radical Muslims coming to power in the region may choose to continue dealing with the West and simply drastically increase prices on everything from Arabian and Central Asian petroleum products to Sudanese and Egyptian cotton and Moroccan oranges in order to sap the economic strength of the West and greatly increase their own wealth, power and influence. Should they wish to deal with nations outside their sphere of influence without coming into contact with the West, the Muslims have the option of trading with Communist North Korea and China. In fact, the Islamic Republic of Iran has a history of doing business under the table with these two nations. The Sino-Iranian alliance, in particular, has proven very fruitful for Iran. China has consistently supported Iran's nuclear program. The Chinese have also sent Silkworm missiles to the Iranians. Similarly, the North Koreans have sent nuclear technicians and military advisors to Tehran. In return, Tehran has supplied "roughly 40 percent of North Korea's oil needs."[19] This, in and of itself, is a good example of the radical Muslims' penchant for establishing valuable bartering relationships. It is highly likely that the productive commercial and military relationships the fundamentalist Muslims in Iran have forged with the North Koreans and Chinese would continue into an era of radical Muslim dominance and control over a large landmass in Asia and Africa.

The military might and scientific and technological know-how of this coming empire will also be substantial. As previously discussed, Iran and the Muslim Central Asian countries have considerable amounts of advanced weaponry, nuclear weapons and conventional military equipment which they inherited or purchased from the old Soviet arsenal. Even now, Iranian air force pilots are learning from their Cuban teachers how to make low-level nuclear bomb runs with their newly purchased MiG-29s[20]. Given the collapse of the Soviet Union and the existence of an active black market in sophisticated military technology, there is no longer any need for

Third World nations to work tediously over long periods of time to develop from scratch their own weapons of mass destruction. Third World armies can quickly become First World nuclear superpowers through black market acquisitions[21]. The Islamic Empire will be a world power literally overnight on land, sea, air and probably in space as well.

It should be noted that the black market acquisition of nuclear weapons by the Islamic fundamentalist powers is not farfetched in the least. As recently as May, 1994, the FBI publicly expressed its anxiety and concern that the newly emergent Russian mafia may be able to steal nuclear weapons from formerly Soviet military facilities for subsequent sale to rogue nations such as Iran, Libya, Sudan and/or North Korea[22].

In terms of weapons maintenance and the upkeep of various military and nuclear facilities, the Islamic fundamentalists have a large reservoir of former Soviet scientists, military personnel and nuclear technicians upon which to draw. A number of former employees of the Soviet military-industrial complex have already moved to Muslim states to work on nuclear, bacteriological and chemical weapons programs and missile technology. We can expect this trend to continue.

Iran, the center of the international Islamic revolution, has made determined efforts since the end of the Iran-Iraq War in 1988 to greatly increase its military capabilities. One analyst recently stated:

> ...President Ali Akbar Hashemi Rafsanjani clearly is determined to expand Iran's military strength...In January, 1990, his government allocated $2 billion per year for five years to buy advanced weapons.

> [T]he scale of Iran's across-the-board military expansion remains impressive. Iran's long-term objective is to acquire a modern air force of roughly 300 advanced combat aircraft (principally Russian-made MiG-29 *Fulcrum*, MiG-31 *Foxhound* and Su-24 *Fencer* fighters and fighter-bombers); a modern army with 5,000 to 6,000 tanks, 2,000 self-propelled artillery pieces, and thousands of armoured personnel carriers; and a navy upgraded with at least three advanced Russian *Kilo*-class submarines and scores of fast patrol boats armed with missiles.

Iran also has purchased hundreds of ballistic missiles and the technology to produce them from North Korea and China[23].

The Muslim world is arming itself at a faster and more determined pace than the West. In 1992, former President Richard Nixon called it "the most militarized region of the underdeveloped world."[24] He noted that "[i]n 1990, the countries of the Muslim world spent a total of over 8 percent of their GNP on the military, while the Western figure was less than 5 percent ... More ominously, the area has become the focal point of the proliferation of weapons of mass destruction and ballistic missiles."[25]

In short, the coming Islamic Empire will be a world power in every sense of the word whose people will share a vibrant religion and a common Islamic culture. Like its Muslim predecessors, the Islamic Empire of the early 21st century will also have an appetite for territorial expansion and military conquest. A modern, worldwide *jihad* against non-Muslim populations and societies complete with nuclear weapons promises to bring the highest casualty rates in the history of mankind. World War III, if it does come, will probably occur between the Islamic Bloc and the Western nations. It will be the deadliest war ever fought by humanity. Given the ability of nuclear exchanges to trigger an effect known as "Nuclear Winter" which would ultimately destroy all life on earth, it may also be the last war ever fought by humanity[26].

§ § §

ENDNOTES

1.   Reuters, March 11, 1993.

2.   Reuters, October 28, 1991.

3.   For a history of oil and its role in the development of the world economy, see Yergin, *The Prize: The Epic Quest For Oil, Money & Power*.

4.   See United Nations, Department of Economic and Social Information and Policy Analysis, *World Economic and Social Survey 1994: Current Trends and Policies in the World Economy*, 135.

5.   Ibid.

6.   Ibid.

7.   Ibid.

8.   United Nations, *World Economic and Social Survey 1994*, 142.

9.   Ibid.

10.   See Yergin, *The Prize*, 588, 698.

11.   United Nations, *World Economic and Social Survey 1994*, 134, Figure V.3.

12.   Ibid., 144.

13.   Ibid., 146.

14.   Ibid.

15.   Ibid.

16.   Ibid., 145.

17.   Halliday, "An Elusive Normalization: Western Europe And The Iranian Revolution," 309, 320.

18.   Phillips, "Saddamization Of Iran," 7-9.

19.   Phillips, "Saddamization Of Iran," 10.

20.   Davidson and Rees-Mogg, *The Great Reckoning*, 223.

21.   See Chapter 1, Section III.

22. "Russian Aide Says Gangsters Try To Steal Atom materials," *The New York Times*, A5 (Thursday, May 26, 1994).

23. Phillips, "The Saddamization Of Iran," 9. See also Joffe, "Relations Between The Middle East And The West," 250, 255.

24. Nixon, *SEIZE THE MOMENT*, 197.

25. Ibid.

26. The devastating meteorological phenomenon known as "Nuclear Winter" which many scientists predict would follow a massive nuclear exchange was first proclaimed and subsequently popularized by noted scientist and Cornell University professor Carl Sagan. Dr. Sagan has discussed the concept on TV and in a number of articles that have appeared in scientific journals, popular magazines and newspapers over the past several years. Put succinctly, scientists who espouse the theory of "Nuclear Winter" believe that a substantial nuclear exchange between nations would not only kill millions in the initial blasts and subsequent release of radiation but would initiate a deadly chain of natural events that would kill off most and possibly all life on earth. These scientists have concluded that multiple nuclear explosions would send huge clouds of dust and smoke into the upper atmosphere that would block out the sun. The jet stream would spread these dust clouds over large parts of the earth. The resulting darkness would disrupt the world's food chain by making photosynthesis impossible for plant life. Worldwide temperatures would also plummet quickly in the absence of the heating effects of the sun. As a result, most and possibly all life on earth would become extinct. The earth would be caught in the grip of a man-made, nuclear induced ice age from which it might take many years to emerge. See generally Fisher, *Fire and Ice: The Greenhouse Effect, Ozone Depletion and Nuclear Winter;* Sagan, *A Path Where No Man Thought: Nuclear Winter and the End of the Arms Race.*

CHAPTER FIVE

THE THREAT AT HOME

The United States is a "den of evil
and fornication.'
-Sheik Omar Abdel-Rahman.
-Frequent refrain heard on hundreds of
the Sheik's "educational" tapes[1].

I will "show all Americans that they'll
never be happy if they don't follow
Islam."
-Sheik Omar Abdel-Rahman
-January 6, 1993[2].

So far, this work has concentrated on explaining the nature of the worldwide threat of Islamic fundamentalism in regions abroad. In this chapter, America's vulnerability to acts of Islamic inspired terrorism and espionage on its own soil will be discussed.

I. Terrorism Arrives in the U.S.

After years of relative immunity, the people of the United States finally fell victim to the plague of terrorism on February 26, 1993. On that date, the World Trade Center in Manhattan was bombed with the loss of 6 lives and injuries to 1,000 people[3]. Property damage and other forms of financial loss caused by the interruption of businesses in the downtown area are estimated to have run into the billions of dollars. Undeterred by some early arrests in the Trade Center case, the group of Islamic radicals who eventually stood trial for these acts boldly proceeded to plot the murder of countless motorists through the planned destruction of two underground tunnels leading out of New York City. They also moved forward with their plan to assassinate U.S. Senator Alphonse D'Amato, a courageous and outspoken critic of Iran and Islamic fundamentalist terrorism, then

U.N. Secretary General Boutros Boutros Ghali and Egyptian President Hosni Mubarak, among others.

James Fox of the FBI has stated that investigators believed that the bombing was masterminded by "a large, well-known terrorist group, a group that knows what it's doing." The presence of Sheik Abdel-Rahman, whose ties to Muslim terrorists in Egypt and the fundamentalist regimes in Iran and Sudan are well-known, certainly suggested an international connection[4]. So too, did the placement of the explosives which destroyed the entire communications and fire control systems in the World Trade Center, broke five of eight electrical feeder cables and caused a flood that disabled the backup generators that were meant to handle such emergencies. The plan for the bombing bore the clear signature of professionals, probably hired by Iran.

While it is true that the World Trade Center bombing was, in the words of Gilmore Childers, Assistant U.S. Attorney, "the single most destructive act of terrorism on American soil," there have been antecedent acts. The assassination of two CIA employees and the wounding of three more on the morning of January 25, 1993 in suburban Virginia by a suspected Islamic terrorist provides still another example of terrorism's arrival on our shores[5]. The party wanted by federal authorities in connection with the killings is an illegal Muslim immigrant named Mir Amir Kansi who had entered the United States illegally and subsequently disappeared after the shootings. Federal authorities believe he fled to Pakistan.

Mr. Kansi holds an advanced degree in English literature from a Pakistan University. Upon arriving in the United States, he nonetheless sought a low paying position with a courier company that made deliveries to the CIA in Langley, Virginia. On the morning of January 25th, Mr. Kansi, age 28, calmly walked with an AK-47 assault rifle in his arms alongside the line of cars waiting to enter the gates at Langley. Immobilized by the rush hour traffic, the CIA workers were easy targets for Kansi as he poured burst after burst of bullets into several of the cars.

The long terrorist arm of Iran and the Islamic fundamentalists has reached deep into the American heartland several times before. On March 10, 1989 a pipe-bomb destroyed the van of Mrs. Sharon Lee Rogers, the wife of the captain of the U.S.S. Vincennes, the American Navy ship that accidentally shot down an Iranian airliner during tensions in the Persian

Gulf on July 3, 1988[6]. Fortunately, Mrs. Rogers was not hurt although her vehicle, which was parked outside the Rogers' San Diego home, was completely destroyed. Investigators determined that the otherwise simple pipe bomb had contained a sophisticated fuse not normally available to members of the public that was activated by heat from the exhaust pipe. No one was ever caught, and the bombing remains unsolved.

The Islamic Republic of Iran's policy of assassinating opposition leaders around the world is well-known. On July 22, 1980, a former senior officer in the Shah's intelligence service named Ali Akbar Tabataba'i was shot by a radical black Muslim posing as a postman making a delivery to his U.S. residence[7]. The assassin David Belfield, otherwise known as Daoud Salahuddin, used a clean handgun and an authentic mail van and mailman's uniform. The killer was immediately spirited to safety by various terrorist groups who shipped him through New York and Montreal to his masters in Tehran.

Iran's terrorist apparatus struck yet again in another quiet American neighborhood on the morning of March 26, 1992. On that date, a woman named Mrs. Parivash Rafizadeh was shot twice outside her home in Franklin Lakes, New Jersey[8]. The contract murder was carried out at close range with a clean .45 semiautomatic pistol which was found nearby. The woman's husband and brother had served in the former Shah of Iran's government. The killer or killers made a clean getaway. Authorities believe that the killing was a professional job carried out by agents of the Islamic Republic of Iran.

Iranian agents have also carried on a years long assassination campaign in Europe. In August, 1991, the harmless and aged former prime minister of Iran Shahpour Bakhtiar was gunned down in Paris[9]. In September, 1992, four Kurdish opposition leaders were killed in Berlin[10]. Since 1987 over a dozen Iranian dissidents living in Europe have been killed by the Islamic Republic of Iran[11].

Fortunately, through good luck and solid police work, several planned terrorist operations have in fact been foiled. Two terrorists posing as respectable Muslim immigrants living in Burlington, Vermont were successfully apprehended on October 23, 1987[12]. Georges Younan and Walid Mourad, two Burlington merchants, waited in a van to rendevous with Walid Kabbani, a Lebanese national living in Canada. Kabbani was scheduled to hike across the Canadian border with a backpack full of bomb components and equipment. These materials would then be used and/or further distributed by Younan and Mourad to other Muslim terrorists living undercover in the U.S. Fortunately for law enforcement authorities, the van in which Younan and Mourad were waiting was illegally parked. When approached by the local police chief, the two acted in a highly suspicious and nervous manner. They were arrested and their rendevous plan was discovered. Unfortunately, no other member of the terrorist network in America was ever exposed.

Some months later on April 12, 1988, another terrorist was arrested by accident on the New Jersey Turnpike[13]. Yu Kikumura, also known as Abu-Shams, was on his way to New York City with a car full of sophisticated anti-personnel bombs and related equipment. Kikumura planned to detonate these bombs in mid-Manhattan around April 15, 1988, the second anniversary of the American bombing of Libya for that country's past sponsorship of terrorism. A member of the Japanese Red Army, a radical Japanese terrorist group, Kikumura had ties with Middle Eastern terrorist groups as well. He had trained with Palestinian and Syrian forces in Lebanon's Biqaa Valley and was on a mission to avenge the bombing of Libya on behalf of his terrorist allies in the Middle East.

Incredibly, Middle Eastern radical groups and state sponsors of terrorism have even made inroads into American gangs in an attempt to recruit individuals to commit terrorist acts on American soil. For example, Chicago's infamous Al-Rukn gang based chiefly on the south side of that city has been implicated in terrorist activities supported and funded by Libya. Four members of the gang were arrested in October, 1986 in Chicago for preparing to conduct terrorist operations in the service of Libya[14]. Such planned operations included shooting down an airplane and blowing up U.S. government buildings. Authorities discovered that the gang possessed an awesome arsenal of weapons for this purpose including machine guns, a rocket launcher and anti-tank and anti-aircraft weapons. Interestingly, the gang's headquarters where the weapons were found was nicknamed "the mosque." A fifth defendant wanted by U.S. authorities successfully fled to Libya. The remaining four were convicted in 1987 of "offering to commit bombings and assassinations on U.S. soil for Libyan payment."

All terrorists by definition represent a danger to the societies in which they operate. Muslim terrorists are especially dangerous given their fanatical world view and willingness to die for their cause. Terrorism expert Bruce Hoffman of the RAND Corp. recently stated:

> The religious terrorist sees himself as an outsider from the society that he both abhors and rejects, and this sense of alienation enables him to contemplate - and undertake - far more destructive and bloodier types of terrorist operations than his secular counterpart[15].

The hijacking of a French Airbus A-300 airliner by AIM, the Armed Islamic Group, in late December, 1994 illustrates the self-abandon of the Muslim terrorist. AIM seeks to overthrow the present military backed government in Algeria, install a radical Islamic government, and purge the nation of all Western influences. The Muslim hijackers planned to blow up the airliner on a suicide mission over Paris[16]. Approximately twenty sticks of dynamite with detonators were found under the plane's passenger seats. In addition, after landing in Marseille the hijackers demanded nearly three times the fuel necessary to fly to Paris, their announced destination. French officials have said that the dynamite plus the extra fuel on board would have destroyed the plane and caused massive destruction and loss of life on the ground had the airliner blown up over Paris, a metropolitan area of 8 million people.

II. America's Vulnerability

How safe are Americans from terrorist attack inside the country? A host of government studies, news reports, magazine articles and specialized reports on terrorism and available counter-terrorist strategies all suggest that Americans are not very safe at all if terrorists are determined to commit further criminal acts of aggression on American soil[17]. Several examples in addition to the terrorist incidents described above underscore this conclusion.

A. Public Parking for Terrorists

Muslim terrorists were able to drive a van packed with explosives into the parking garage of the World Trade Center, the site of the spectacular explosion which destroyed several underground floors of that building, because that building's parking garage was completely open to the public. The World Trade Center is not unique in this regard. Many large commercial buildings make their parking facilities freely available to members of the public on a drive-in basis. There is no need to purchase a parking sticker, undergo a cursory identity check, or prove that you are a tenant of the building or are visiting a tenant.

In 1983 an anti-terrorist task force specifically informed the Port Authority of New York and New Jersey that the World Trade Center's parking garage was vulnerable to bomb attacks and recommended that it be closed to the public[18]. The Port Authority rejected the recommendation thereby enabling Islamic terrorists to succeed in blowing up part of the building ten years later with the loss of 6 lives. The Port Authority's executive director, Mr. Stanley Brezenoff, has stated that his agency will now consider restricting public access to the garage as well as other measures to enhance public safety and security.

B. Easy Access to Nuclear Power Plants

Other incidents are also extremely troubling. In early 1993, a man succeeded in gaining access to a civilian nuclear power plant by crashing his station wagon through a fence at the Three Mile Island nuclear plant in Pennsylvania[19]. This incident underscores the ease with which a determined terrorist driving a truck of powerful explosives could conceivably blow up a domestic nuclear facility anywhere in the U.S. thereby triggering the widespread release of deadly radioactivity.

Civilian nuclear power plants in the U.S. are not particularly noted for their armed security staff. Gaining illegal entry to such facilities has never been a major challenge for protesters or extremists of any stripe, whether they are rock stars or environmentalists protesting the use of nuclear energy (the pop singer Jackson Browne is famous for breaking into nuclear power plants) or emotionally disturbed individuals who crash the gates for less apparent reasons. In the wake of the Three Mile Island incident and the World Trade Center bombing, the United States Nuclear Regulatory Commission ("NRC") has stated that it will re-assess the threat that truck bombs pose to nuclear reactors[20].

C. Don't Drink the Water

In addition to nuclear power plants, there are a plethora of other public installations (e.g., dams, electrical power plants, bridges, water treatment plants, reservoirs) which present ripe targets for terrorists. Attacks on such installations would be generally easy to execute given the unguarded or minimally secure nature of most of these facilities. Attacks on these targets have the added attraction of causing significant disruption on a state-wide or even regional basis. To cite just two examples of the kind of disruption that could be caused by an attack on America's water supply, one has only to recall the problems New York City and Milwaukee had with bacteria in their municipal water supply in 1993[21].

In April, 1993, citizens of the city of Milwaukee were forced to boil their water or buy bottled water after it was discovered that a waterborne disease called cryptosporidiosis had infiltrated the water system. This disease crippled tens of thousands of people with flulike symptoms and killed several who were elderly, suffering from AIDs or were otherwise in poor health. Similarly, New York City suffered the second water scare of the year in the summer of 1993 when bacteria turned up in the tap water of several Manhattan establishments. The problem was corrected and the City ultimately blamed "bird droppings" for the incident. Both incidents demonstrate the ease with which the U.S. water supply can be compromised. There is no need for an individual terrorist or terrorist nation to invent an exotic disease to be unleashed upon the American public. One need only discreetly pour a bacterium that can remain viable and multiply in tap water into a reservoir in order to disrupt an entire city. There are many such "low-tech" techniques available to terrorists.

D. Shopping for Explosives

Obtaining explosives is also a relatively easy task. The FBI has speculated that the truck bomb that blew up in the World Trade Center was made, at least in part, by publicly available fertilizer[22]. More conventional explosives are also easy to come by. Purchases of dynamite and other explosives are not well monitored[23]. More than 4.1 billion pounds of explosives are sold in the United States each year. While purchasers must complete a form detailing their criminal and psychological histories, there is currently no procedure in place for verifying the accuracy of purchasers' representations in this regard. Thus, it is an easy task for convicted felons, illegal aliens, terrorists and others to buy explosives. There have been 30 thefts of explosive material of at least 300 lbs each throughout the country in the last four years. This constitutes a large supply of firepower illegally held by persons unknown. Of course, terrorists can also smuggle across the border their own supply of weapons and explosives.

E. Terrorists in Our Midst

The terrorist problem is unavoidably made worse by the fact that ours is an open society which places a premium on individual freedom and liberty. Terrorists cynically take full advantage of the freedoms afforded by our democratic society in order to undermine and destroy it. They have also used America as a staging ground for operations against other countries. As a result, terrorist groups have generally operated and moved about freely in our country with little fear of arrest or detention from the authorities unless "caught in the act" of planning or carrying out a terrorist attack.

We know that the radical Muslims accused of the World Trade Center bombing were either naturalized U.S. citizens or had slipped into the country illegally under the noses of the Immigration and Naturalization Service ("INS") and United States Department of State[24]. According to a chronology provided by the U.S. State Department and other facts compiled by Representative Olympia Snowe of Maine, alleged ringleader Sheik Omar Abdel Rahman was able to enter the United States five times since 1990 even though his name had been on the State Department's watch list of potential security risks since 1987. Furthermore, the Sheik was still in this country actively preaching hatred and violence against non-Muslims even though his visa had been revoked in November, 1990. The sheik is just one notable example of a suspected terrorist who has passed with ease through the federal government's security net into the United States. Who knows how many other Islamic terrorists have slipped into this country.

As previously mentioned, the World Trade Center suspects have had their predecessors. In early 1989 the FBI's second in command at the time, Mr. Oliver Revell, testified before the Senate Foreign Relations Subcommittee on Terrorism, Narcotics and International Operations that members of Iran's radical Revolutionary Guards had entered the United States posing as students[25]. Revell estimated that there were about 200-300 Iranian nationals living in the U.S. as students. He believed that of that number perhaps several "tens" were members of Iran's fanatical Revolutionary Guards.   Mr. Revell complained that once these Iranian agents had successfully entered the country, it was very difficult to expel them under current law.   Similar stories have circulated in the press including a rumour that the radical Islamic terrorist group Hezbollah (purportedly responsible for holding Western hostages in Lebanon during the 1980s) held an organizational meeting in the American Midwest during the 1980s without the knowledge of or surveillance by federal law enforcement authorities[26].

Several foreign governments have publicly complained that terrorist groups have used the United States as a staging base for their activities in the Middle East and elsewhere[27].   For example, it has been alleged that Hamas, the Palestinian terrorist group which opposes peace with Israel, runs its terror network not from a shadowy, well-fortified bunker somewhere in Lebanon but from its offices in suburban Virginia[28].   The German, Israeli and French intelligence agencies all have stated to members of the press that senior leaders of the terrorist groups Hamas, the Moslem Brotherhood, Islamic Jihad and leaders of Algeria's militant Islamic opposition group the FIS not only visit but live for extended periods of time in the United States.   Incredibly, according to the testimony of a Hamas terrorist arrested in 1993 in Israel, senior officials of that Islamic terrorist group held a workshop in Chicago for new terrorist recruits from the American Muslim community on how to build a car bomb.   In the Trade Center case itself, the Egyptian government repeatedly warned the U.S. about the threat to public security presented by Sheik Rahman and complained that the Sheik was working to overthrow the Mubarak regime (as he had worked against Anwar Sadat's government) from his base of operations in a Jersey City mosque.

These troubling examples are undoubtedly just the "icing on the cake." It is estimated that tens of thousands, perhaps even several hundred thousand, illegal Muslim immigrants enter the United States *each year* without the knowledge or consent of federal authorities. We simply do not know how many of the thousands of Muslim illegals currently living in the United States are actually terrorists bent on organizing underground cells and orchestrating acts of violence in the U.S. We also do not know for certain what proportion of the hundreds of Iranian and Sudanese "students" who we have graciously permitted into this country so that they may take advantage of our educational system are actually Islamic radicals planning our destruction. According to a report published in the March 6, 1989 issue of *US News & World Report*, out of a population of approximately 30,000 Iranian students studying in the United States, the Tehran regime can rely on a core group of 1,000 to conduct acts of terrorism against America and its civilian population if so asked. The World Trade Center bombing and public statements from federal law enforcement officials and foreign intelligence agencies on the subject of domestic terrorism strongly suggest that these immigrant and student groups may contain a number of dangerous terrorists.

This tense and dangerous situation is not helped by the hundreds of audio tapes, video cassettes and English language Muslim newsletters which circulate within some quarters of the American Muslim community and which spout a virulent brand of racial, ethnic and religious hatred against Jews, Americans, Western society, etc.[29] These materials were found by the boxload in the living quarters of the Trade Center defendants and at Sheik Rahman's mosque. The sheer volume of this hate literature has been characterized as "substantial" by members of the media who have investigated it. The content is all very disturbing as well. For example *Khillafah Magazine*, an English language monthly that is published in London but disseminated in many American mosques, routinely prints articles calling upon Muslims to "confront" the West through violence. Furthermore, the anti-Semitic sentiments expressed in print and on several of the tapes would make the most fervent Nazi proud. Islamic terrorist groups also spread their message of hate and violence against Jews, Westerners and other non-Muslims via cable-television. The expatriate Lebanese Shiite community living in Dearborn, Michigan is able to watch regular rebroadcasts of Hezbollah's fiery propaganda on Channel 23, the local community-access cable channel. These programs are full of hatred for Israel and the United States. In one program, a video of Hezbollah soldiers firing Ketusha rockets at an Israeli settlement plays while a voice urges acts of violence against Israel and the United States.

While an entire immigrant community should not be tarred with a single brush, the existence of this kind of programming and the apparent popularity of tapes, newsletters, videocassettes and TV shows which preach violence against the West only hurts the cause of Muslims seeking to peacefully coexist with their non-Muslim neighbors in the U.S. Responsible leaders within the American Muslim and Arab communities should condemn, not defend, excuse or otherwise protect, the kind of hate mongering contained in the materials and programming mentioned above. Allegedly religious materials which actually preach murder and other assorted acts of violence, glorify killing and espouse a stridently racist and anti-Semitic viewpoint have absolutely nothing to do with religion as most citizens of the world would define that term.   Certainly the venerable religion of Islam does not appear to condone or compel such behavior. Indeed, Islam was notable during the Middle Ages and during later time periods for its tolerance of the local Jewish and Christian communities which existed within its borders.   This historical record of tolerance, at roughly the time of the Spanish Inquisition and European wars of religion, is an historical fact of which all Muslims should be proud. Islamic leaders in America and around the world should say as much and should firmly distance themselves from the Islamic fringe.

§ § §

ENDNOTES

1.   "A world terrorist link?" *The Hartford Courant*, C1 (Sunday, June 20, 1993).

2.   "Egyptian Jihad Leader Preaches Holy War To Brooklyn Muslims," *The Wall Street Journal*,   A1, A5 (Wednesday, January 6, 1993).   The reader will note that the newspaper's interview with the radical sheik took place prior to the World Trade Center bombing. It appears that Sheik

Rahman attempted to keep his word. The bombing killed 6 Americans and injured or maimed 1,000 others.

3.   "The New Terrorism," *Newsweek*, 18-23 (July 5, 1993). See also *The New York Times*, March 9, 10, 1993; *The New York Post*, March 8, 1993. The author drew additional facts concerning many of the terrorist incidents discussed in this section from Bodansky's excellent and thoroughly documented book *Target America: Terrorism in the U.S. Today*. See also Bodansky, *Terror! The Inside Story Of The Terrorist Conspiracy In America*; Revell, "Protecting America," 3-8.

4.   Vincent Cannistraro, former head of the CIA's counterterrorism operations, has gone so far as to state that Sheik Rahman has long been funded by Iranian intelligence. Phillips, "Saddamization Of Iran," 8.

5.   Wootten, "Terrorism: U.S. Policy Options." See also *The New York Times*, January 26, February 10, 11, 1993.

6.   *The New York Times*, March 11-13, 1993; *The Los Angeles Times*, March 11, 1993.

7.   Kupperman and Kamen, *Final Warning*, 47.

8.   *The New York Times*, March 28-29, 1992.

9.   Phillips, "Saddamization Of Iran," 8.

10.   Ibid.

11.   Ibid.

12.   Kupperman and Kamen, *Final Warning*, 10; *The New York Times*, January 28, May 18, 1992; *The Wall Street Journal*, February 11, 1988.

13.   Kupperman and Kamen, *Final Warning*, 10-12, 84; *Newark Star Ledger*, February 5, 1989.

14.   *Chicago Tribune*, November 7, 1986; *Chicago Sun Times*, December 30, 1987; *Washington Times*, August 19, 1992.

15.   Wright, "New Breed of Terrorist Worries U.S.," *Los Angeles Times*, A5, A7 (June 28, 1993).

16.   Kraft, "Plane wired to explode, France says," *The Hartford Courant*, A1, A6 (Wednesday, December 28, 1994); Hedges, "France Wages a Lonely Battle with Radical Islam," *The New York Times*, Section 4, E5 (Sunday, January 1, 1995).

17.   Sources consulted regarding America's vulnerability to domestic terrorism and available counter-strategies include John M. Collins, Senior Specialist in National Defense, "Transnational Terrorism And Counteractions: A Primer," *CRS Report for Congress*, Congressional Research Service, The Library of Congress, Washington, D.C.: March 18, 1993; James P. Wootten, Foreign Affairs and National Defense Division, "Terrorism: U.S. Policy Options," *CRS Issue Brief*, Congressional Research Service, The Library of Congress, Washington, D.C. July 22, 1993; Department of State Publication, "Patterns of Global Terrorism: 1992," Washington, D.C., April, 1993; Laurence Pope, Acting Coordinator for Counter-Terrorism, Statement before the Senate Judiciary Committee, Washington, D.C., April 21, 1993, "Department's Efforts To Combat International Terrorism," Vol. 4, No. 17 *US Department of State Dispatch*, April 26, 1993; Office of Technology Assessment, "Technology Against Terrorism: The Federal Effort," *OTA Report Brief*, Reproduced by Congressional Research Service, The Library of Congress, July, 1991; Oliver Revell, "Protecting America," *Middle East Quarterly* II, no.1: 3-8; "A New Strain of Terrorism," *Washington Post*, A1, A14 (August 3, 1993); "New Breed of Terrorist Worries U.S.," *The Los Angeles Times*, A5, A7 (June 28, 1993).

18.   *The New York Times*, B5 (March 1, 1993).

19.   "A-Plant Security May Rise," *The New York Times*, B4 (March 4, 1993).

20.   Ibid.

21.   Sara Terry, "Drinking Water Comes to a Boil," *The New York Times Magazine, The New York Times*, Sunday, September 26, 1993.

22.   "The New Terrorism," *Newsweek*, 18, 20 (July 5, 1993).

23.   *The New York Times*, A1, A20 (March 2, 1993).

24.   "Shock Waves," *NATIONAL JOURNAL*, 25:1349-1352 (June 5, 1993).

25.   "Iran Guards in U.S., FBI Says," *The New York Times*, A6 (March 9, 1989). Mr. Revell also repeated many of his claims and warnings concerning Muslim terrorist penetration and activity inside the United States on an autumn,1994 broadcast of the television news program "60 Minutes."

26.   "A world terrorist link?," *The Hartford Courant*, C1, C4 (Sunday, June 20, 1993).

27.   Ibid.

28.   *The New York Times*, Section IV, 5 (February 21, 1993).

29.   "A world terrorist link?," *The Hartford Courant*, C1, C4 (Sunday, June 20, 1993).

CHAPTER SIX

DOMESTIC TERRORISM: A Plan Of Action

"The public must always remain
vigilant against acts of terrorism to
ensure that terrorism does not become
commonplace in this country as it has
in many other countries."
-William S. Sessions, then-Director of the FBI.
-FBI report on terrorism released in 1993[1].

I. America's Wake-Up Call

Recent terrorist acts underscore the dire and immediate need for a constructive plan for combatting terrorism. The World Trade Center bombing initially prompted some politicians and journalists to ponder the risk of future terrorist acts directed at American citizens and installations. But that introspection largely ceased in the months and years subsequent to the bombing as many Americans returned to the comfortable, if now outdated, notion that they were safe from terrorist attack as long as they stayed within the U.S. border.

America's political leaders at both the state and federal levels should initiate a dialogue with the American people about the nation's vulnerability to terrorism at home. Hearings should be called and an analysis conducted of the risks of terrorism on U.S. soil. After conducting a comprehensive analysis, the President and members of Congress as well as the mayors of our major cities should come forward and present to the American people, to the degree possible without compromising national security, a range of credible options for reducing the terrorist threat.

In addition to safety, cost is obviously a factor that needs to be taken into account. There are several relatively cheap, cost effective measures that can be taken immediately[2].

II. Enhanced Security/Greater Public Education

Counter-measures against terrorism need not be particularly "high-tech" or expensive. Increasing the general public's awareness of the terrorist threat and requiring buildings and facilities over a certain size to institute additional safeguards to enhance security would represent significant steps in the right direction. (These steps also would have the beneficial effect of lowering insurance rates for these businesses and buildings.) For example, the World Trade Center and many other large commercial buildings around the country should heed the recommendations made in 1983 to the Port Authority of New York and New Jersey that public parking and access to certain facilities be restricted.

The security of public transportation facilities should also be reassessed. Cars should not be allowed to park or idle in heavily trafficked areas such as bus or airport terminal entrances. Furthermore with respect to air transportation, baggage on all domestic and international flights should be precisely 'matched' with every passenger known to be on board a given airplane before that aircraft disembarks from the gate, as is the practice of several European and Middle Eastern airlines. This will help ensure that a terrorist will not be able to plant a bomb in a piece of luggage while escaping to safety. If such controls had been in effect in December, 1988, the destruction of a Boeing 747 over Lockerbie, Scotland most likely would not have taken place.

A little public education on the subject of terrorism can go a long way toward reducing the risk of a successful terrorist attack. Public safety messages can easily be posted in subways, airports, bus terminals and other public areas warning commuters to be on the lookout for unattended baggage and unmanned vehicles parked in prominent or heavily travelled areas. U.S. television stations have run ads urging youngsters to avoid drugs. Former First Lady Nancy Reagan launched a highly publicized and well regarded public service program against drugs commonly known as "Just Say No." America could easily produce a set of low-budget public service announcements urging citizens to be alert for unattended bags or packages in public places or cars parked or abandoned for a long time in a busy thoroughfare or shopping area.

At present, America entirely lacks even a rudimentary program for educating the public about ways to spot and avoid a potential terrorist incident. By contrast, public education programs are currently operational in several European nations including Great Britain. These programs have enabled the general public to assist the authorities in spotting suspicious behavior or situations before disaster strikes. Finally, a short, inexpensive and focused program in the public school system on identifying terrorist behavior would also be helpful in sensitizing the nation's youth to this threat to their safety and well-being.

III. Immigration Reform

The federal immigration laws themselves and the way those laws are enforced and administered by the United States Immigration and Naturalization Service and the United States Congress are also partly responsible for the terrorist threat we face in this country. Something is clearly wrong when a feeble, blind and elderly cleric like Sheik Abdel Rahman is able to pass freely back and forth into the United States without being challenged or questioned despite the fact that his name appeared for several years on the State Department's 'watch list' of suspected international terrorists. According to Congresswoman Olympia Snowe (R-Me), Sheik Rahman entered the United States at least five times since 1990 despite the fact that his visa had been revoked[3]. How could this have occurred? What can be done to prevent this from happening again?

First and foremost, certain aspects of the INS itself must be reformed. On February 15, 1989, the U.S. Department of Justice released a scathing 34 page audit of that agency[4]. The Justice Department concluded that the INS was poorly run, terribly disorganized and incapable of effectively carrying out its mission. Multiple problems were cited. A few are briefly recounted here in order to give the reader a flavor for the Justice Department's findings. The auditors found that the INS'S Miami regional office had lost a grand total of 23,059 citizenship and nationalization certificates. These certificates prove U.S. citizenship and are actively traded on the black market for large sums of money. This number of lost certificates is absolutely mind boggling and either demonstrates gross incompetence or constitutes circumstantial evidence of corruption on the part of INS workers in that office.

Furthermore, in an examination of 51 citizenship cases, the Justice Department found that in "virtually 100%" of the cases the required background checks and fingerprinting had not been carried out with respect to aliens who were in fact granted the privilege of becoming U.S. citizens. Many fraud investigations were also not being carried out. Finally, the auditors determined that the INS did not consistently follow legally required procedures in handling citizenship applications, holding immigration hearings and the like.

These problems are serious and cannot be overlooked. Yet, in all fairness not every immigration problem or shortcoming can be laid at the INS'S doorstep. The INS has fewer agents than the immigration and border patrol services of many European countries. As a result, the agency has had a difficult time keeping up with the tremendous challenges it faces daily. More INS agents have to be hired and then placed at border locations such as airports in order to intercept illegals when they step off the plane. These agents also need to be handed fast and accurate intelligence regarding suspected terrorists so that suspects can be quickly identified, detained and then ultimately excluded from entering the United States. According to the Immigration Act of 1990, suspected terrorists can be legitimately denied entry into the United States based on national security grounds. We need to give our INS agents the right information so that they can effectively utilize this legal mechanism.

The federal immigration laws should be amended and asylum procedures should be modified in order to strengthen the federal government's ability to summarily exclude or deport aliens who it believes pose a danger to the security of the United States and its citizens[5]. Currently, while the federal immigration laws provide the INS with several weapons for quickly denying non-citizens entry into the country (assuming such malcontents are actually identified while attempting to enter the U.S.), the tools for deporting aliens who are already here are slow, laborious and woefully inadequate. Non-citizens can spend years contesting attempts to deport them. This buys precious time for terrorists and their supporters in this country. The Immigration Act of 1990's deportation procedures should be streamlined and the grounds for deportation expanded where appropriate. It should not take years to deport suspected terrorists who have somehow been able to enter this country illegally.

At the very least, federal authorities should have somewhat enhanced powers to detain and sequester suspected terrorists for whatever period of time is necessary to protect the public's safety. Terrorists should not be out on the street while waiting for their next court date. In one particularly notorious example, a Muslim terrorist was allowed to roam freely in this country while waiting for a hearing on whether he would be granted political asylum[6]. Ramzi Ahmed Yousef arrived at Kennedy International Airport in New York from Pakistan without a valid visa. He claimed that he was seeking political asylum. The INS determined that the local immigration detention center was already filled to capacity and therefore released Yousef onto the streets of New York City. He was informed of a hearing date concerning his application for political asylum and directed to appear on that date. He never showed up for any of 3 hearings that were scheduled on his behalf. Yousef later allegedly helped carry out the World Trade Center bombing that killed 6 people. The FBI subsequently placed him as No. 1 on their Ten Most Wanted List and offered a $2 million reward for his capture. He eluded authorities for two years until an informer unexpectedly walked into the American Embassy in Islamabad, Pakistan, disclosed the fugitive's whereabouts and collected his reward[7]. Yousef was finally captured and deported back to the U.S. in early February, 1995.

Several bills dealing with immigration reform have been introduced in Congress. In the 103rd Congress, former Rep. Romano Mazzoli (D-Ky) introduced House Resolution 1679 which was designed to amend the Immigration and Nationality Act's provisions regarding asylum. He also introduced House Resolution 2602 which was intended to improve immigration enforcement, enhance anti-smuggling capabilities and authorize appropriations for the Immigration and Naturalization Service. Similar measures have been touted by other members of Congress including Rep. Olympia Snowe (R-Me).

IV. Monitoring the Purchase of High Explosives

The previous chapter demonstrated the ease with which explosives can be purchased or stolen. There is a way to counter these problems. More thorough background checks should be made of purchasers of explosive materials. This will greatly reduce if not completely eliminate the problem of purchases by criminals and illegal aliens who have snuck into this country. These records should not remain with the seller or explosives dealer but should also be logged into a central data base for easy access by state and federal authorities. Next, better records should be required of all explosive manufacturers, distributors, retailers and storage facilities. Enhanced recordkeeping will deter theft at each of these facilities. Finally, U.S. lawmakers should consider requiring that all explosives contain an indestructible, color-coded plastic chip or tag that could allow investigators to trace an exploded device back to its place of purchase and ultimately to the purchaser. This idea was first surfaced in the early 1980s by the U.S. at the time of the terrorist crisis with Libya. It was initially rejected due to the cost involved for manufacturers. In the wake of the World Trade Center and Oklahoma City bombings, the idea of "tagging" domestic explosives may be an idea whose time has come.

On the international scene at least, nations have in fact required that certain compounds be added to explosive agents in order to reduce the risk of future terrorism. For example, after the Lockerbie disaster in 1988, the U.S. led a successful international effort to add a vaporous agent to all plastic explosives. Bomb sniffing dogs can be trained to detect this chemical agent. In addition, American and European firms are working on developing a machine that would detect this agent. American lawmakers should think creatively along these lines in dealing with the danger posed by the sale and use of explosives.

V. Restore the Office of Counterterrorism

In the wake of the bombing of the Marine Corps barracks in October, 1983 in Beirut, Lebanon and the terrorist threats against the life of the American president emanating from Libya, President Reagan created a new State Department post to coordinate counterterrorist strategy on the part of the entire U.S. Government[8]. The post, Coordinator for Counter-Terrorism, carried ambassadorial rank thus ensuring that inter-agency and inter-office rivalries on terrorism issues further down in the federal bureaucracy could be successfully overcome. Whoever filled the position also had easy access to members of the Cabinet and senior executive branch advisors by virtue of their civil service rank. President Reagan's brainchild was a much needed step in the right direction. Unfortunately, the Clinton Administration has downgraded the office and fired or reassigned much of its seasoned staff[9]. America's ability to identify and address terrorist threats and formulate effective counterstrategies on a timely basis has suffered as a result. In the wake of the World Trade Center bombing and the escalating rhetoric of the Islamic fundamentalists, the counterterrorism office should be restored to its former status and position in the executive branch.

§ § §

ENDNOTES

1.   Terrorist Research and Analytical Center, Counterterrorism Section, Intelligence Division, Federal Bureau of Investigation, U.S. Department of Justice, "Terrorism in the United States 1982-1992," U.S. Department of Justice, Federal Bureau of Investigation, Washington, D.C. 1993.

2.   A good single source discussing available counterstrategies for combatting terrorism is Collins, "Transnational Terrorism And Counteractions: A Primer."

3.   "Shock Waves," *NATIONAL JOURNAL*, 25:1352 (June 5, 1993).

4.   *The New York Times*, A9 (March 4, 1989).

5.   Revell, "Protecting America," 3, 7.

6.   "A New Strain of Terrorism," *Washington Post*, A1, A14 (August 3, 1993).

7.   "Behind Arrest of Bomb Fugitive, Informer's Tip, Then Fast Action," *The New York Times*, A1, B2 (Friday, February 10, 1995).

8.   "Counterterrorism: Victim of Success?," *Newsweek*, 22 (July 5, 1993).

9.   Ibid; Phillips, "The Saddamization Of Iran," 11.

CHAPTER SEVEN

DEALING WITH THE THREAT FROM ABROAD

"Today we have no protection from
even a single ballistic missile."
-Ambassador Henry F. Cooper, former
Chief U.S. Negotiator at the Geneva
Space and Arms Talks and Director of
the Strategic Defense Initiative
Organization.
-July 7, 1993[1].

"It is clearly and completely wrong"
to believe that SDI is obsolete and no
longer necessary due to the end of the
Cold War.
-Dr. Edward Teller, former member of
the President's Foreign Intelligence
Advisory Board and one of the world's
most prominent nuclear scientists.
-September 21, 1993[2].

America's approach to national security during the years 1945-1990 is not
necessarily the appropriate approach to take in the greatly changed
post-Cold War period. The federal government has only begun to realign
its defense strategy, military budget and acquisition programs to meet the
threats posed by this new, dangerous and extremely disorderly post-Cold
War world. A bewildering array of potential enemies has made it difficult
for America and its NATO allies to reorient their land, air and sea-based
nuclear weapons. Who should we target in the hopes of deterring an
aggressor, assuming effective deterrence is even possible? What should be
the theoretical foundation of America's defense policy given the ominous
rise of Islamic fundamentalism and the likelihood that nuclear missiles and
other weapons of mass destruction will continue to proliferate and change
hands around the world?

This chapter will analyze and discuss current U.S. defense policy, explain why Cold War defense strategies may no longer work in the post-Cold War world and will suggest a new approach to defense which holds out the greatest prospect of success regardless of the source of a military attack against America and the West.

I. Cold War Defense Theory

America's Cold War defense strategy was founded upon the closely related theories of containment and deterrence[3]. Out of these sprang the strategy of mutual assured destruction or MAD. The theory of containment posited the notion that Communism was inherently hostile to and incompatible with democracy and therefore must be contained worldwide. State Department employee George Kennan first articulated what would become America's policy of containment in a written communication he sent back to the United States from his diplomatic post in Moscow. Kennan's containment theory would later be formally articulated in his famous 1947 article "The Sources of Soviet Conduct" published in *Foreign Affairs* that summer[4].

And what was the best way to contain the Soviet Union's ongoing workers' revolution? Several approaches were tried, discarded and tried again by successive U.S. Administrations in the years between 1945 and 1990. However, the underlying concept of deterrence, that is to say deterring the Soviet Union from an expansionist foreign policy, has always served as the cornerstone of all of these approaches. Simply put, the United States and its Western allies have always held out the threat that force would be met with force and that the Communist bloc would be punished for taking any aggressive actions which threatened Western interests. This 'stick' has at times been pared with a 'carrot' which promised that if the Communist world reduced its military presence in Eastern Europe and its military capabilities and hostile activities worldwide, the West would respond in kind with a reduction in military tensions. This last strategy, which came to be known as detente, was introduced most prominently during the Nixon-Kissinger era. During the 1970s, the United States and the Soviet Union were able to agree to certain limits on their Cold War competition. These arms race limitations were eventually embodied in the Strategic

Arms Limitation Treaties ("SALT I" and "SALT II") and other diplomatic initiatives.

The theories of containment and deterrence quickly ripened by the 1950s and 1960s into the military policy of mutual assured destruction or MAD. Pursuant to MAD, the United States as a matter of defense policy stated that it would launch a massive, all-out nuclear strike if it became the target of a Soviet nuclear first strike or if the Soviet Union launched a large scale, conventional force invasion of Western Europe. MAD was invoked with respect to a potential conventional force invasion of Western Europe because the nations which belonged to the North Atlantic Treaty Organization ("NATO") at the time, the anti-Communist military alliance consisting of the U.S. and most Western European nations, lacked the military might to repulse a Soviet Bloc invasion by conventional means. Therefore, the West needed to articulate a credible threat to deter possible Soviet designs and ambitions with regard to Western Europe.

MAD in particular and the theory of military deterrence in general worked as a defense strategy because in the final analysis the Soviets could be counted upon to act rationally in weighing the pros and cons of an attack upon the West. Presumably, they considered the destruction of their own country and the extermination of large numbers of their people in deciding how to behave militarily. Both the Soviet Bloc and the Western allies obviously placed significant value upon their cities, culture, population and military and commercial installations because for 45 years the Cold War never erupted into a nuclear "hot war." Both sides weighed the horror of total war in the nuclear age and, to their credit, ultimately acted with military restraint.

II. The Limits of Deterrence

In contrast to the Cold War adversaries described above, religious fanatics cannot be deterred. It is impossible to deter a Muslim fundamentalist who believes that his passport into heaven is to attack a Western citizen, city or installation and die in the commission of such an act. The only way to 'deter' such fanatics is either to kill or imprison them or foil their terrorist plans prior to commission. Death is meaningless to a religious zealot who believes fervently in a glorious afterlife and that the surest guarantee for reaching heaven is to achieve martyrdom fighting the infidel.

What are the implications for Western security caused by this new and dangerous threat? The rise of a hostile, violent and aggressive form of Islam throughout Asia, Africa and the Middle East means that the cornerstone of postwar American national security policy - the concept of deterrence generally and MAD in particular - may be largely obsolete. Deterrence is only minimally effective against religious fanatics and should never constitute the sole strategy for protecting the peoples and nations of the West. The coming Islamic Empire is not going to be easily dissuaded from attacking the West by the possibility that scores of Western missiles may be unleashed in self-defense or retaliation against Islamic soil. The greater the suffering, the greater the eternal glory for Muslims in their holy war against the non-Muslim world. If anything, the Islamic Bloc may cynically count on certain civilized norms of behavior existing within the West which will tie the hands of the Western allies and prevent them from responding effectively in kind.

When viewed in light of their behavior to date, a strategy of deterrence against Muslim fanatics like the Islamic fundamentalists does not appear promising. The Iranians were capable of sustaining mind numbing casualties while prosecuting their eight year war with Iraq from 1980-1988. The Islamic Republic of Iran also demonstrated that it had no moral qualms against kidnapping young boys from playgrounds and soccer fields and sending them to run across mine fields in front of Iranian military units in order to detonate any hidden mines. The political and religious leadership in Tehran justified this practice as guaranteeing the young victims entrance into heaven. Given the history of violence in the region, some of the more thugish leaders in the Middle East appear to consider life less dear.

In a similarly brutish vein, Saddam Hussein committed genocide against unarmed Kurdish villagers in northern Iraq, starved his Shi'a citizens in the south and, during the Gulf War committed the worst act of environmental terrorism in the history of mankind when he sabotaged the oil facilities throughout the country of Kuwait during the Iraqi retreat. Hussein was absolutely undeterrable in the months leading up to the war with the West in 1990-1991 despite overwhelming evidence that he would be defeated in battle. Saddam Hussein's behavior demonstrates the limited utility of a strategy of deterrence. We can expect more leaders out of Hussein's mold (most likely wilier and smarter than the somewhat oafish Hussein) in the future from the Middle East.

III. The Need to Develop an Effective Ballistic Missile Defense

In the absense of deterring an Islamic military attack outright through the display and deployment of Western nuclear and conventional military capabilities, America and other Western governments will need to develop other means for effectively protecting their citizens, culture and civilization from destruction. Iran's purchase of advanced Soviet weaponry, including missiles, long range bombers and submarines, and its apparently successful attempts to hire poverty stricken Soviet scientists to maintain and upgrade those weapons, means that a fundamentalist Islamic regime bitterly hostile to America and the West will soon have the technological capability to carry out nuclear, biological and chemical strikes against the continental United States and other Western nations. This is something which radical Middle Eastern leaders such as Saddam Hussein, Khomeini, Khaddafi and others have implicitly and explicitly boasted about and threatened to do for some time. Up to this point, the West's political leaders and press organs have largely ignored such threats because these dictators lacked the means of carrying them out. With the collapse of the Soviet Union, the existence of an active black market in Soviet military technology and the proliferation of weapons of mass destruction around the world, such leaders may soon be able to carry out their barbaric threats against the U.S., Israel and other Western nations. Based on past experience, chances of successfully deterring such leaders or their successors in that part of the world from attacking other nations are not great.

A deliberate nuclear, biological or chemical missile attack against America and the West could also originate from outside the Islamic world. For example, relations between China and the West have not thawed since the Tianeman Square massacre in 1989 and may grow worse depending upon whether Communist China treats Hong Kong roughly after it takes possession of that city in 1997 and whether relations between China and Taiwan continue to worsen to the point of possible military conflict[5]. The brunt of China's nuclear arsenal is currently pointed at the United States and Russia. At the same time, an intransigent, paranoid and isolated North Korea is stubbornly forging ahead with its own military nuclear program and the means to deliver nuclear warheads via a long range missile, currently under development, which possesses a 2,000 to 6,000 mile range called the Taepo Dong 2^6. Other nuclear wannabes include Iran, Libya, Algeria, Syria and, most likely Iraq, despite the UN imposed sanctions against the latter country. After the Gulf War it was discovered that Iraq was within eighteen months of developing nuclear weapons for deployment on its ballistic missiles[7]. The inability of the International Atomic Energy Agency (IAEA) to discover Iraq's nuclear program prior to the Gulf War despite regular inspections of that country and Iraq's pledge to remain nuclear free as a signatory of the Non-Proliferation Treaty (NPT) underscore the profound weaknesses of any international nuclear "arms control" regime. Diplomacy and arms control agreements unfortunately do not work in every instance.

The worldwide proliferation of weapons of mass destruction appears to be an intransigent problem that only grows worse with the passage of time. Rather than attempt to identify every possible American adversary and aim some relatively small portion of our nuclear arsenal at every one of these nations (with no guarantee of deterring that adversary from launching an attack in any case), it makes sense from both a military and economic perspective to construct a defensive shield against all aggressors.

The risk of a deliberate missile strike against U.S. soil is compounded by the possibility of accidental or unauthorized nuclear launches. According to a former Soviet general whose remarks appeared in the February 2, 1990 issue of *Pravda*, even before its ignominious collapse the Soviet Union did in fact launch a nuclear tipped missile accidentally[8]. Fortunately, the engine misfired and the missile crashed only a short distance away from its launch site without detonating its nuclear cargo[9]. With the collapse of the Soviet Union, many nuclear weapons systems may eventually degrade to the point where they are no longer safe for their operators to handle and may present a mortal risk to those inhabiting their intended, pre-selected targets. The vast majority of these targets lie in the West. Senators Nunn and Lugar, among others, are especially concerned about this problem. The two visited Moscow in December, 1992 in an effort to address the problem of control over Soviet nuclear missiles and came back troubled by the risks that the Soviet nuclear arsenal still posed to America and its allies[10].

Russian officials have recently disclosed the existence of a Soviet "Dooms-day Device" capable of launching massive nuclear strikes against the West automatically without human intervention or support. These reports were carried by many Western media organs in the autumn of 1993 and appear credible. The Soviet Doomsday Device poses a continuing threat to America and its allies. This system may degrade to the point that it accidentally self-activates or it may fall into the hands of terrorists who might use it for nuclear blackmail. Hostage taking, kidnapping and other terrorist incidents have risen dramatically in the former Soviet Union since the collapse of Communist authority and control. It is at least possible that elements of the Soviet arsenal including the so-called Doomsday Device may fall into the hands of thugs, terrorists or blackmailers. In point of fact, the FBI publicly stated in May, 1994 that it fears the Russian mafia may get its hands on Soviet nuclear weapons or materials and use them for blackmail or sell them abroad.

Another compelling reason for deploying some form of missile defense that may at first glance appear far-fetched is the threat posed by asteroids on a collision course with earth. This little known danger has recently received more attention as scientists have discovered thousands of asteroids of different sizes in orbits that cross earth's own. The great asteroid impact in Siberia in 1908 (which released energy equivalent to a large nuclear explosion) and the giant, miles-wide crater in Arizona made by an ancient asteroid impact attest to the tremendous destructive force that is unleashed when one of these rocks hits the earth. A ballistic missile defense would be capable of launching a killer missile at one of these threats from space in time to destroy the asteroid or knock it into a new and non-lethal trajectory. The respected British newsmagazine *The Economist* ran a cover story entitled "The threat from space" in September, 1993 on this very subject. That periodical stated:

> An impact as big as the Siberian one might be expected roughly once a century. Much larger bodies, a mile or so across, may hit the earth every few hundred thousand years. What they lack in frequency, though, they make up for hand-somely in ferocity. These larger impacts would throw vast quantities of muck into the upper atmosphere, reflecting back sunlight and cooling the ground. In the cold and dark below, crops would fail and billions might starve.

A report in America's Congress in 1992 by a panel of experts said that if there were such an impact, a quarter of the world's population would die[11].

The Economist calls the expenditure necessary to protect against the threat of asteroids "trivial" when compared to the amount of money society spends protecting against other natural disasters like hurricanes, tornados, earthquakes and the like. Admittedly, an asteroid collision and a missile attack have two major differences that would affect to some degree the engineering approaches taken to divert the threat. An asteroid has a mass that is orders of magnitude larger than a typical missile. Second, an asteroid will provide days or even months of warning while a missile attack provides seconds to minutes. Countermeasures for a missile attack require high acceleration and partial destruction. Countermeasures for an asteroid require high velocities and diversion.

While not the sole rationale for exploring anti-missile technology, the danger to humanity posed by asteroids constitutes at least another reason for further research into this general field.

The Europeans, Israelis, Japanese and Russians are all clearly worried about the problem of nuclear proliferation and the risk of a deliberate or accidental nuclear launch[12]. For example, Marshall Shaposhnikov, the Commander in Chief of the Commonwealth of Independent States ("CIS") Combined Armed Forces stated in a February 12, 1992 Russian news article:

> The thing is that we have nonetheless reached the point where roughly a dozen or more countries could shortly join the nuclear club. We will have less and less reliable insurance against breaches in the rules of storage and protection and unsanctioned use of nuclear weapons in various regions[13].

So what can be done to counter all of these risks? America and its allies should continue to research, test and develop ballistic missile defense technology with the goal of eventually deploying a system that can protect large areas of the earth such as North America and Europe. Marshal Shaposhnikov, in the same article quoted above, stated that his country had reached the same conclusion. Shaposhnikov concluded "all this convinces us that it is time to think about a global defense system" along the lines of the Strategic Defense Initiative ("SDI"). Similar statements were made by other CIS and Russian officials leading up to Russian President Boris Yeltsin's historic proposal announced on January 31, 1992 that America and Russia build and jointly operate an SDI-type space-based missile defense system. Distracted by the upcoming presidential election, the Bush Administration did not actively pursue President Yeltsin's offer. Unfortunately, the Clinton Administration has been philosophically opposed to a space-based missile defense system for some time. While the Clinton Administration has largely turned its back on ballistic missile defenses for the American people, many other developed nations have expressed an interest in constructing such a defensive system, either jointly or alone.

Given the lead time involved in developing sophisticated defensive systems of this sort, no time should be wasted in continuing R&D programs in the area of missile defense. The biggest military blunder the United States of America could ever make in the immediate post-Cold War period is to virtually abandon any serious effort to develop a credible ballistic missile defense system capable of protecting millions of Americans from a deliberate or accidental nuclear attack. This is exactly what President Clinton and the American Democratic Party have done in first deriding and then, once in control of both the executive and legislative branches of government after the 1992 U.S. presidential election, moving swiftly to dismantle research, gut funding and destroy public support for SDI, which was first announced by President Reagan in March, 1983[14]. In the words of former U.S. Ambassador, senior arms control negotiator and weapons expert Henry F. Cooper:

> The Clinton Administration appears intent on delaying any serious [ballistic missile defense] acquisition program for the US homeland until the threat is clearly apparent to all. This could be a fatal mistake for many Americans[15].

At the present time, the United States Government can offer its citizens absolutely no protection against any petty despot, tinpot dictator or terrorist who decides to build, buy or steal a nuclear missile and launch it against an American city.

IV. Ballistic Missile Defense: The Manhattan Project of Our Time

A. The Manhattan Project Analogy

The development of a comprehensive space based and/or land based ballistic missile defense system is, quite simply, the Manhattan Project of our time. During the early 1940s, President Roosevelt in a moment of vision decided to fund an unproven and highly controversial engineering project that would eventually lead to the successful development of the atomic bomb. Amazingly, the supersecret Manhattan Project was at least partly initiated by an unsolicited letter sent by Albert Einstein to the White House stating his belief that nuclear energy could be harnessed as a power source and developed into a usable weapon[16]. (Dr. Einstein had fled Europe by the start of the war and was then spending most of his time at Princeton University in New Jersey.) Einstein's letter and the exigencies of war soon led to the formation of a formal government program.

Doubters easily outnumbered the core group of individuals who believed that America's scientific and military communities could meet the exciting challenge of developing and harnessing nuclear power. Critics attacked the program as unsound science, derided the concept of nuclear power as beyond mankind's capabilities and poked fun at the idea of exploiting nuclear energy as something out of a science fiction fantasy novel. It was also argued that a nuclear development project would drain valuable funds from the rest of the war effort. But Roosevelt proceeded in spite of the skeptics. With the A-bomb, America and its allies were virtually guaranteed success against the Axis powers. Ironically, after the war it was confirmed that Nazi Germany had been working along the same lines. If the German nuclear program had received more timely support from Adolf Hitler, Nazi Germany may have won the race to develop the A-bomb and subsequently won the war.

Like America and its allies in the late 1930s and early 1940s, America and its Western allies again face a mortal threat posed this time by the proliferation of nuclear weapons worldwide. Many of these weapons of mass destruction are falling into the hands of the West's avowed enemies, chief among them the violent and unpredictable Islamic fundamentalists. For these reasons, America and its allies should proceed with the development and augmentation of ground based and/or space based anti-missile systems.

Throughout history, the military hardware introduced in a previous conflict generally presages the machinery to be used on a larger scale during the next conflict. The introduction of the rickety and somewhat unreliable biplane and submarine during World War I led to German wolf packs and massive Allied bombing campaigns twenty five years later during World War II. Similarly, helicopters used in Korea came to dominate the battlefield in Vietnam. The use of the American Patriot missile against the Iraqi Scud during the 1990-91 Gulf War provides a glimpse of the shape of wars to come. We should heed the lessons of that war and prepare our forces to fight a high-technology, missile dominated war on a much larger scale. The Gulf War was a success story for American built and operated sophisticated military hardware.

The deployment of the Patriot along the battle front during that war demonstrated the ability of corporate America, working together with the government, to develop a sophisticated and highly advanced defensive system capable of knocking incoming missiles from the sky. America cannot afford to lose confidence at this late stage in its scientific and technological abilities as a nation. The United States, along with other military partners, must build and deploy a defensive shield capable of protecting Americans from nuclear attack.

SDI has had the support of some of the world's greatest scientific minds. Dr. Edward Teller, one of the world's most distinguished nuclear scientists who worked on the Manhattan Project and went on to many other professional achievements, is an ardent proponent of ballistic missile defense research and technology. Dr. Teller was an early believer in the technical viability of the Strategic Defense Initiative, popularly known as "Star Wars," which was first announced by President Reagan in March, 1983. During the 1980s, he had the opportunity to study the ballistic missile threat and the concept of constructing a comprehensive ballistic missile defense as a member of the President's Foreign Intelligence Advisory Board. Dr. Teller has strenuously argued against the Clinton Administration's dismantlement of the research programs which support anti-missile defense technology and has bemoaned the misguided belief that there is less risk of a nuclear exchange now that the Cold War is over. The reality is quite the opposite. Unfortunately, as Henry F. Cooper, a former senior U.S. official, arms control negotiator and ballistic missile defense expert, has stated, SDI and its successor ballistic missile defense systems are now not "politically correct" in Washington.

General Chuck Horner, a senior field commander during the Gulf War, has also advocated further research and development of missile defenses. Reflecting on his experiences during the 1991 conflict, General Horner has identified some holes in Allied defenses and sees a need to upgrade and deploy a Patriot-type anti-missile weapon on a much larger scale to protect Allied forces deployed in an entire theater of conflict. General Horner stated in a 1991 issue of **Aviation Week**:

> I underestimated the political impact of the Scud -- a lousy weapon...a miscalculation...diffused only by the success of the Patriot...Patriot's success has also exposed a hole in the allied arsenal. Patriot is a point defense weapon...areas to be defended in Saudi Arabia are concentrated in a few small clusters. If the allied military targets had been spread out, there wouldn't be enough Patriots in the world to defend them all... When very accurate warheads are available to third world nations, the US will need a regional wide-area air defense force to duplicate on a grand scale the Patriot's pivotal role of defanging the Scud[17].

Thus, an upgraded missile defense system is needed both to protect Western military forces deployed over a wide area in the field of battle and to protect civilians from missile attack.

B. Can Ballistic Missile Defenses Work?

1. Combining Existing Technology in New Ways

As with any highly sophisticated piece of technology, there are some who believe such a piece of equipment can work and some who believe it cannot. Dr. Teller and scientists who have worked on the government's SDI program are greatly encouraged by what they have seen and tested so far. Unlike America's research into nuclear energy during World War II or the current worldwide search for "cold fusion" today, the development of a comprehensive, wide area ballistic missile defense is largely a function of combining known technologies in new ways. For example, in greatly simplified terms a ballistic missile interceptor is a conventional missile armed with a computer chip brain which can "recognize" and steer the defending missile toward an incoming enemy warhead. Recognition of the enemy warhead can be accomplished by inserting heat sensors capable of reading the heat signatures of other objects in the sky or space. This can be coupled with related technology such as an electronic "eye" or other instruments that permit an airborne missile to identify moving objects by size, electronic signal, visual markings, etc.. These recognition systems can also be installed together on the same missile in order to complement one another.

A defending missile also needs to counter an enemy warhead's evasive movements (called "countermeasures") with its own. Again, existing technology can be installed and upgraded where appropriate to accomplish such a task. As envisioned, a missile defense system would be supported by orbiting surveillance satellites which could notify a ground based military command center of any suspicious missile launches as well as activate the defense system automatically upon detecting a missile headed toward protected territory. Existing reconnaissance satellites currently in space or due to be launched in the near future can easily fulfill this function.

2. SDI and Its Successors

SDI as originally conceived would have been a space-based missile defense system capable of countering a massive nuclear strike. One or more unmanned satellites would first detect a nuclear launch and then destroy the incoming nuclear warheads before they reentered earth's atmosphere. SDI was criticized primarily because of the logistical difficulties involved in simultaneously tracking and destroying upwards of several hundred ballistic missiles at once. Furthermore, SDI contemplated the use of laser technology, known as space-based lasers, to track and destroy enemy missiles. Such technology was still experimental at the time and largely unproven in this context in the early 1980s.

The SDI concept and supporting government programs have undergone several changes and modifications in the last 13 years[18]. The extensive use of laser technology was later replaced with the idea of deploying "killer" missiles, called space-based interceptors, mounted to and launched from the orbiting satellites themselves. This was the heart of the Brilliant Pebbles concept, which was a somewhat pared down successor to SDI. The project contemplated several orbiting platforms loaded with killer missiles capable of destroying a smaller number of ballistic missiles than would ordinarily be involved in a massive attack. Brilliant Pebbles seemed more suited to the post-Soviet era of smaller individual nuclear adversaries, China notwithstanding. Global Protection Against Limited Strikes ("GPALS"), the last government anti-missile program which was announced during the Bush Administration, is designed to do just what its title suggests - confer wide area, global protection against only limited nuclear strikes.   Again, GPALS would seem to be an appropriate response to the threat of deliberate, unauthorized or accidental nuclear launches. Unfortunately, the Clinton Administration and its Democratic allies in Congress have been staunch opponents of any protective anti-missile system for the American people. As recently as December, 1994, Clinton Defense Secretary Perry rejected Republican calls to revive an SDI-type missile defense program for the protection of the American public.

3. Tested in Battle

Some skeptics have attacked the missile defense concept by asserting that such a defense lies beyond the boundaries of humanity's present technological capability. This statement is demonstrably false. In a very real sense, missile defense technology has already been tested, deployed and used successfully on the battlefield. Theater missile defense ("TMD") systems were used with great effect during the Gulf War. The Patriot missile shot down numerous Soviet made SCUD missiles in Saudi Arabia and Israel thereby protecting large numbers of Allied ground forces in Saudi Arabia and local civilians in both Saudi Arabia and Israel. The success of the Patriot prevented significant Israeli casualties and enabled the Western allies to convince Israel to stay out of the war. There can no longer be any doubt that missile interceptor technology works. The Navy's AEGIS system, untested in the last war, represents yet another TMD that can be expanded and improved upon to provide wide-area missile defense.

A large scale missile defense system for large parts of North America and Europe would essentially require upgrading and expanding the tried and battle tested technology found in the Patriot and the already deployed AEGIS system.   The Gulf War represented a triumph for American technology and demonstrated that the West still has the technological "edge" over the Soviet-made weapons systems deployed against it. What the West must do now is keep that edge by pushing ahead with a program of ongoing research and development in the field of missile defense just as the West's adversaries are even now pushing ahead with research into improving their nuclear launch and delivery capabilities.

4. Ballistic Missile Defense Tests: A Success or Failure?

The U.S. military conducted several tests of SDI technology throughout the early to mid-1980s that demonstrated the viability of such a system[19]. The 1984 Homing Overlay Experiment or HOE program demonstrated that so-called Kinetic Kill Vehicles or KKV's could hit objects in space that travel at the same velocity as an incoming ballistic missile. ICBMs move at about 7 km/sec above the earth's atmosphere. In several HOE tests, ground based missiles destroyed orbiting targets moving at this velocity. The former Soviet Union's modern long range missile, the CSS-2, travels even more slowly than that at a speed of only 5 km/sec. Therefore, given the proper financial and political support to deploy such a system, the U.S. military appears perfectly capable of countering the threat of nuclear weapons mounted on Soviet built missiles.

In another crucial experiment conducted in 1985 the United States Air Force launched a missile equipped with electro-optical sensors from an F-15 fighter jet. The missile successfully destroyed a dying U.S. satellite in space. This again proved that America already had the technical know-how by the mid-1980s to build missiles that could destroy incoming warheads in space. Since the 1980s, the interceptors have gotten progressively smaller and more advanced. In the words of Henry Cooper, former Director of the SDI Organization and former Chief U.S. Negotiator at the Geneva Space and Arms Talks, "the technical challenge" of building a space-based ballistic missile defense system "is the easiest part of the problem." In fact, "we are a decade beyond proof-of-principle."

5. Leaving the U.S. in the Dust

Ironically, while the United States under Ronald Reagan first popularized the SDI concept, other nations have since moved ahead of America in terms of supporting such a program. The "believers" include the Europeans, Israelis, Japanese and Russians, each of whom is seriously interested in developing a ballistic missile defense system of its own. Significantly, we now have solid and entirely credible evidence that during the final decade of the Cold War the Soviets themselves believed that SDI would work. Mr. Vladimir Lukin, Russia's Ambassador to the U.S. and formerly Chairman of the Supreme Soviet Foreign Relations Committee, publicly stated that the Soviet Union was very fearful that SDI would be successfully deployed and operated. He expressed his belief that Ronald Reagan's SDI program actually shortened the Cold War by at least 5 years[20].

Today, Soviet fears about the feasibility of SDI technology have been replaced by Russian enthusiasm for a joint Russian-American program to develop a ballistic missile defense. Not finding any takers in the Clinton Administration, the Russians have forged ahead with their own research into ballistic missile defenses. In particular, they are apparently working to develop a defense system capable of knocking down their own CSS-2 long range missiles. For example, while traveling abroad American Ambassador Henry F. Cooper witnessed a marketing briefing by a Russian scientist in Erice, Italy in which the scientist asserted that the Russians could develop a defensive system to defeat their own CSS-2 missiles for a few hundred million dollars. In light of this evidence of Russian eagerness to work with or for others in designing anti-missile technology it is quite possible that the Russians will eventually reach agreement with the European community or others to jointly develop and operate a missile protection system. A Russian-European venture would leave the U.S. out in the cold and completely unprotected by whatever missile shield might be eventually deployed.

V. The Russians Extend Their Hand

On January 31, 1992, Russian President Boris Yeltsin made a stunning and visionary offer to the United States:

> I think the time has come to consider creating a global defense system for the world community. It could be based on a reorientation of the U.S. Strategic Defense Initiative to make use of high technologies developed in Russia's defense complex[21].

This invitation to cooperate on missile defense matters was later repeated by President Yeltsin in a number of different fora. The most recent Russian position echoes President Reagan's earlier offer during the mid-1980s to Soviet President Gorbachev to share SDI with the world in order to prevent nuclear war.

The Russians are clearly worried about nuclear proliferation generally and the nuclear and military threats rising on their southern flank in Iran and the breakaway Muslim republics in particular. The Russian position is itself a product of an evolution in Soviet thinking about these same problems[22].

By 1990 and 1991, the Soviets were concerned that Third World nations possessing nuclear weapons would be less affected by deterrence considerations than the United States and NATO in deciding whether to use those weapons. They therefore began to ponder joint development with other nations of a wide-area missile defense system. Unfortunately, the American government has yet to take the Russians up on their offer. Yet, there are compelling reasons for pondering joint development of such a system with one or more nations.

A. Spreading the Costs

One of the chief objections to the development of a ballistic missile defense (apart from engaging in the fantasy that there aren't any ballistic missiles pointing at us because the Cold War is over) has been the huge cost. This is an important and oft-repeated criticism but one to which there is an easy answer. Joint development, maintenance and operation of a land-based, sea-based and/or space-based ballistic missile defense system in conjunction with one or more countries would significantly reduce the economic cost of such a venture to any one nation. Joint development would also allow the U.S. and Russia to take a scientific "shortcut" toward development by using one another's research and technology. The Russians are clearly more familiar than we are with the inner workings of their Soviet-built nuclear missiles. Working together with them, we could more easily develop an effective system capable of identifying, targeting and destroying these warheads before they reach their targets.

The American-Russian partnership might eventually be expanded to include several European nations as well as Japan, Canada and Mexico. Depending on the scope of the protective shield, operation and control of such a system might be located at one or more ground positions in each hemisphere. For example, a missile defense system deployed over North America or the North Atlantic might be operated at an American military installation. A system deployed to protect Europe and Russia may be operated and controlled from a NATO or Warsaw Pact base or from ships stationed in the North Sea and Mediterranean Sea.

Never before have so many diverse nations located around the globe faced the same, catastrophic threat from nuclear weapons. This common problem presents a wonderful opportunity to forge an effective, worldwide alliance against the use of weapons of mass destruction. The interest of so many nations in countering this threat to mankind also permits the U.S. and its allies to spread the cost of developing and deploying a ballistic missile defense system among several participating nations, thereby reducing the expense for any one country. The supposed financial burden associated with developing a ballistic missile defense system, touted so often by critics, thus can be easily overcome. Given the need for such a defense and having run out of any substantive excuses for not proceeding with research and development in this field, the U.S. Government should waste no time in forging ahead in this area.

Inevitably, some nations protected by the missile shield will be what is known in economics as "free riders" - meaning that they will reap the benefits of protection without paying for it. For example, El Salvador might be protected from an accidental or deliberate launch of a weapon of mass destruction by the eventual deployment of a "North American Missile Shield." Yet, that nation is probably too poor to pay for this protection. This situation should not present a problem since enough larger and wealthier nations exist in every hemisphere to split into relatively manageable sums the cost of deployment and maintenance. In addition, small nations might be asked to make a small, token payment, commensurate with their national ability to pay, which would further defray the cost of a ballistic missile defense in their hemisphere.

Given the indications of political instability inside Russia, the U.S. and its allies may ultimately decide to accept only on limited terms Russia's offer of joint development of a missile defense system. The important point is that Russia and other nations think an SDI-type missile defense system can be developed and are interested in cooperating in this area. Given Iran's huge purchases of Soviet missiles and other weaponry, the United States should not waste this historic opportunity to learn from the Russians about Soviet missile capabilities. Furthermore, if other dependable allies are willing to work with America and help defray the costs associated with such research, then such steps should be encouraged and explored.

B. The ABM Treaty

The Anti-Ballistic Missile ("ABM") Treaty of 1972 presents yet another apparent roadblock to the U.S. Government's development and deployment of wide area missile defense systems. The United States and the Soviet Union signed and ratified the ABM Treaty which prohibits the two countries from deploying anti-ballistic missile systems (launchers, interceptors and related equipment such as radar) against strategic ballistic missiles except in very limited circumstances. These limited exceptions are set forth in Article III of the Treaty and essentially permit the two nations to protect their respective national capitals from missile attack and to protect their ICBM silos in the same way. The allowable anti-ballistic missile systems are limited by Treaty both in terms of the size of the effectively protected area (measured in kilometers) and the amount of ABM hardware that can be used by each country. Apart from those narrow exceptions, the two signatories have pledged themselves according to Article V "not to develop, test or deploy ABM systems or components which are sea-based, air-based, space-based or mobile land-based."

The Treaty is of infinite duration according to Article XV. However, that same article provides that either signatory can withdraw from their commitments under the Treaty upon giving the other party six months' notice accompanied by a written explanation as to why the party has elected to withdraw.

It is true that the 1972 ABM Treaty and its associated protocols would appear to prohibit the development of wide area missile defense systems on the scale and of the type advocated here. However, it is equally true that the ABM Treaty provides a mechanism whereby the United States or the successor states of the former Soviet Union, the latter of which have said publicly that they consider themselves bound by such international

132 Anthony J. Dennis

treaty agreements signed by the Soviets, can easily withdraw from some or all of the Treaty's obligations. There are no restrictions on withdrawal other than giving six months advance notice. Such an act is completely voluntarily and may be exercised at any time.

As has been demonstrated, Russia and many other countries have publicly expressed their desire to develop some form of effective wide area missile defense system. Therefore, there is little doubt that Russia and probably many of the other C.I.S. countries would welcome or at least be indifferent to Washington's announcement that it was withdrawing from the ABM Treaty in light of the looming threat posed by the spread of nuclear weapons and the need to develop ABM systems to protect against that threat. Indeed, it is possible that Russia or one of the other Soviet successor states may beat the U.S. to the punch and make this declaration of withdrawal on its own without U.S. participation so that it can pursue missile defense technologies in conjunction with other countries.

In a *de facto* sense, the Russians repudiated the ABM Treaty years ago when their predecessor state, the Soviet Union, built the football-size Krasnoyarsk early warning radar system to detect incoming missiles and developed and deployed SA-10 and SA-12 anti-missile systems as well as S-300 and S-500 interceptor systems[23]. The Russians have never felt inhibited by the ABM Treaty from developing and deploying anti-missile systems. Indeed, the Soviets never even bothered to consult with the Americans regarding whether a particular ABM-type system is or is not prohibited by the treaty[24]. As a result, the citizens of Russia, particularly those in and around Moscow, can rest easy at night knowing that they are protected by the world's most extensive anti-missile system. The citizens of the U.S. deserve no less.

The actions of the Clinton Administration stand in stark contrast to the Soviets and Russians with respect to the interpretation of and compliance with the ABM Treaty. Instead of exploiting the ambiguities inherent in the ABM Treaty (for example, only ABM systems designed to defend against "strategic" ballistic missiles are prohibited, yet the term "strategic" is left undefined), the U.S. has slavishly adhered to the strictest possible reading of that treaty[25]. As a consequence, America's anti-missile programs have been needlessly retarded while other nations, including Russia, continue to move ahead in this regard. Furthermore, the U.S. has steadfastly looked the other way while first the Soviets, then the Russians, installed ABM-type systems that on their face appeared to violate the ABM Treaty[26]. Why the U.S. adheres to such a disadvantageous double standard is mystifying in light of the worldwide proliferation of nuclear weapons and the missiles that carry them.

C. Capturing the Moral High Ground

There is one other, more intangible but no less important advantage that would be conferred on the Western democracies if they chose to seriously pursue the development of an SDI-type missile defense system. Such a system would enable the West, in its delicate, nerve wracking and protracted conflicts with the Muslim fundamentalists, to capture the moral high ground from these religious radicals because the system is a defensive not an offensive one.

The radical Muslims are well known for their paranoia and their tendency at times to believe in fantastic conspiracy theories such as the rumour repeated inside Iran that the C.I.A. actually killed Egyptian President Anwar Sadat, America's avowed ally. (Many other factually unsupportable and wildly improbable stories could be repeated here). A number of these radical religious leaders also exhibit some sign of suffering from a persecution complex, not an infrequent personality trait among religious zealots. This is a dangerous situation for the West since virtually anything the Western nations do to try to address the rising security threat posed by the fundamentalist Muslims may be perceived as an aggressive attack on the movement.

A missile defense system would enable the West to protect itself without needlessly provoking the Muslim fundamentalist revolutionary movement. SDI is, after all, strictly a defensive weapon. It cannot harm others, only prevent harm from being visited upon those who deploy it. It will be hard under such circumstances for Tehran or Khartoum (or possibly Cairo, Istanbul and Algiers in coming years) to allege that the West was arming provocatively against it.

Such a defensive system also does not discriminate or single out Muslim nations, another beneficial aspect of the program. Missile defenses would protect against missile attacks originating from anywhere on the globe.

Thus, the radical Muslims could not claim that this was a weapons system aimed specifically at them. The system, as mentioned in a previous chapter, would have the added advantages of protecting against 1) accidental launches, 2) attacks from non-Muslim states like Communist China and North Korea and 3) attacks orchestrated by terrorist or organized crime groups from anywhere worldwide. At the same time, it must be admitted that the troubling statements emanating from places like Khartoum and Tehran are at least partly responsible for any eventual decision further to develop and deploy missile defense technologies.

In order to underscore its peaceful intent, the United States should seriously consider publicly adopting a "no first use" policy concerning the military use of nuclear weapons. With the disappearance of the threat of a massive Warsaw Pact invasion of Western Europe (which NATO could not credibly deter with solely conventional forces and hence had to make at least rhetorical use of nuclear weapons) there seems to be no reason why the United States should delay making such a public announcement to the world.

VI. The Collapse of American Security?

An impressive array of senior military and civilian officials from prior Democratic and Republican Administrations, some of the world's most distinguished scientists and the governments of a number of technologically advanced countries besides the United States are all convinced that constructing a ballistic missile defense is an idea whose time has come. Unfortunately, the current Administration is loathe to admit either the need for or the feasibility of a ballistic missile defense system. SDI and its successor programs have been a favorite target of the Democratic Party throughout the 1980s and 1990s. This destructive habit has proven hard for the Left to overcome. Political attacks on SDI were a favorite hobby of liberal pundits who gleefully dubbed the program "Star Wars" in an attempt to paint President Reagan as a starry-eyed dreamer lost in a science fiction fantasy. But it appears that Reagan may have once again been on precisely the right track all along. The Russians, Europeans, Israel and Japan certainly seem to think so.

Despite the ominous developments within the Muslim world, the loss of strict, centralized control over the awesome Soviet nuclear arsenal, the ongoing weapons bazaar in the former Soviet Union and the alarming proliferation of long range missiles and weapons of mass destruction worldwide, the Clinton Administration and its Democratic allies (who until the November, 1994 elections controlled Congress for approximately half a century) are reluctant to admit to themselves or others that a military program largely initiated and supported by the Republicans represents the best method for protecting our troops in the field and our citizens at home from missile attack. As Ambassador Henry Cooper has publicly stated, ballistic missile defense is not receiving support because it is still not "politically correct" in Washington to stand up and actually speak in favor of such a program. Fortunately, that situation appears to be changing in the wake of the 1994 Congressional elections.

A. A Critique

Ambassador Cooper, Dr. Edward Teller, Admiral Elmo Zumwalt, USN (Ret.) the former Chief of Naval Operations, General John Foss, USA (Ret.), Rear Admiral Robert H. Spiro, USNR (Ret.) and other defense experts from both major American political parties have all publicly criticized the Clinton defense budget, including the absence of R&D funds for continued anti-missile research[27]. This roster of critics is notable not only for the impressive credentials that each of these individuals possesses but also because several of these senior officials served in prior Democratic Administrations and/or are active members of the Democratic Party. For example, Rear Admiral Spiro served as Under Secretary of the Army during the Carter Administration. Admirals Zumwalt and Spiro have both been active within the Democratic Party. Yet, such is their concern for the safety and security of the American people that they chose to publicly criticize in a highly visible fashion the defense budget of a sitting Democratic President. Far from providing America with a smaller, lighter, flexible fighting force, these defense experts have charged that the Clinton defense budget leaves America with a "hollow force" incapable of fighting two regional wars at once, despite the self-serving statements made by the Clinton Administration.

B. America the Vulnerable

As a longtime weapons expert, arms negotiator and former Director of the SDI program, Ambassador Henry F. Cooper had some choice words for President Clinton's decision to drastically cut funding and support for ballistic missile defense in the face of mounting nuclear threats worldwide:

> [T]he world is still a dangerous place; in some regards, more dangerous than in the Cold War...I am concerned that the Clinton Pentagon made substantial cuts in the [ballistic missile defense] budget I left behind....These cuts mean that:
>
> * Some very important theater missile defense programs will not receive the attention they should - notably Navy wide-area theater defenses and Air Force boost-phase defenses;
>
> * There will be no serious acquisition program to defend the American people, leaving them totally vulnerable to ballistic missile attack; and
>
> * It will be difficult to sustain the necessary technology programs to assure that we can stay ahead of the inevitable [technology race].
>
> I strongly believe that the administration's dismantling of all acquisition programs to defend the American people is imprudent. I do not believe there is any basis for confidence that the United States could not be threatened with at least a limited ballistic missile attack before we could have provided a defense even under the plan I left behind...The Clinton administration appears intent on delaying a serious acquisition program for the US homeland until the threat is clearly apparent to all. This could be a fatal mistake for many Americans[28].

In a speech before the US Strategic Command at Offutt Air Force Base in Nebraska in July, 1993, Ambassador Cooper stated:

> I cannot resist ... pointing out that a space-based interceptor system is the most versatile, affordable global defense option

for providing world-wide protection against ballistic missiles with ranges more than a few hundred miles. Unfortunately, such a system is not now "politically correct," and its serious pursuit simply is not in the cards for at least 3 1/2 years, barring some mind-changing internationally redefining event[29].

The Clinton team's strong opposition to the concept of missile defense does not bode well for the safety and security of American soldiers and citizens facing a rising radical Islamic threat at the end of the twentieth century.

VII. Diplomatic Measures

Diplomatic measures to stem the spread of weapons of mass destruction and to undermine political and material support for Islamic fundamentalists in Iran, Sudan and around the world are necessary and important steps, but they are not sufficient in and of themselves.

Diplomacy can only go so far in protecting Western interests. One has only to recall the existence of Iraq's secret nuclear weapons program that existed despite the fact that Iraq was a signatory to the Non-Proliferation Treaty (NPT) and therefore had pledged itself both to inspections by the International Atomic Energy Agency (IAEA) and to not develop nuclear weapons, to see that diplomacy, international arms control guarantees and monitoring by international agencies have their limitations. Former U.S. Ambassador to the United Nations Jeane Kirkpatrick phrased the problem with diplomacy this way:

> The problem with the 'arms control approach' to security is that the same governments against whom we most need protection are those most likely to violate treaties[30].

Economic sanctions are another frequently invoked measure both in the United Nations and in the halls of Congress. Who can doubt that if the United States and its Gulf War allies had punished Iraq solely with economic sanctions instead of military force that Iraq would still be in Kuwait today?

Some rogue states will simply be uncontrollable through diplomacy and economic sanctions and will continue to build or acquire weapons of mass destruction until they are physically prevented from doing so through military conflict[31]. The West thus has a choice: engage in what might be styled a preventive war or construct and reorient its own defenses in anticipation of facing greater nuclear threats in the future. As Michael Mandelbaum has stated in his provocatively entitled article in *Foreign Affairs* "Lessons of the Next Nuclear War," "a preventive war ...has neither a basis in international law nor a well-established historical precedent."[32] Hence, this book has chosen to emphasize defensive measures such as SDI.

Nonetheless, diplomatic measures are valuable first steps in the war that the Muslim fundamentalists have declared on Western nations and Western society. The United States must continue to work with other peaceful nations around the world to limit the spread both of weapons of mass destruction and ballistic missile technology and weaponry. The former goal is the objective both of the NPT and of an informal group of countries known as the Nuclear Suppliers Group[33]. The second goal is the objective of another informal group created in 1987 called the Missile Technology Control Regime. These groups can slow but probably not stop the spread of the above mentioned technology. The United States should also exert pressure on China to stop selling Silkworm missiles and other nuclear and advanced military technology to Iran and North Korea. The West should observe a trade embargo and economic sanctions against Iran, Sudan and any other country that goes fundamentalist, until such time as those nations renounce their literal and rhetorical war against the West and its citizens. The United States will have to take the lead in this effort since France and Germany seem eager to renew and expand their substantial commercial and diplomatic contacts with Iran at the soonest possible moment. These two nations must be convinced of the folly of their actions.

In terms of official policy vis-a-vis the Muslim fundamentalists, the United States and its allies should make it clear at all times that it has no hostility toward or reservations about the religion of Islam as such. Rather, the Western allies should only express serious reservations about and work to oppose those groups known as fundamentalists who use a radical interpretation of Islam as justification for a policy of hatred and violence against the West and all non-Muslims. This is essentially the policy the United States announced through former Assistant Secretary of State Edward Djerejian in June, 1992 which has come to be known as the Meridian House Declaration[34].

Islam is not the enemy. Although there are social and political aspects of that religion which diverge from salient features of Western society those factors have not and should not be an absolute bar to friendship between the Muslim and non-Muslim worlds. There are moderate interpretations of the religion, for example those put forth by Taha who was swiftly and brutally executed without what most would consider a fair trial by Sudan in 1985 for apostasy, that have enabled Muslim regimes to co-exist peacefully with their neighbors and with non-Muslim nations such as are found in Europe and the Americas. Unfortunately, according to the words and deeds of its leaders, fundamentalist Islam has declared itself to be the implacable enemy of the West. It is this extreme version of Islam, a strain which would be most brutal to its own people in enforcing norms of social behavior and which would be most hostile to Western interests, that is ascendant in the Islamic world. If the Muslims unite politically it will be under the fiery banner of fundamentalist Islam, not the moderate banner of liberal democracy or any other ideology not native to that region of the world.

The West must not get caught in the web of its own rhetoric when talking about democracy or religion. The fundamentalist movement has very astutely taken hold of democratic slogans in pushing for free elections in those troubled countries where they have become powerful. They seek to beguile the West into betraying its allies in Africa and the Middle East and to join the fundamentalist call for free elections at the earliest possible point. But supporting the fundamentalist call for elections in places like Algeria because that is the "democratic" thing to do is not ultimately supportive of democracy. In fact, in joining the fundamentalist call for elections, Westerners will merely have helped the Muslim extremists to hijack democracy for their own ends. Iran has not had a truly free election since the mullahs seized control in 1979. Sudan does not have a democracy either. There is very little doubt, given their anti-Western rhetoric (and even anti-democratic rhetoric in unguarded moments), that the Muslim fundamentalists would never permit a plural and democratic political system to exist once they attained power.

The West must not fall into the trap of unwittingly supporting radical Muslim attempts to use democracy today in order to betray democratic principles tomorrow. Instead, as in Eastern Europe and the former Soviet Union, the United States and its allies should work toward the formation of those institutions and ideals which make a democracy work in the long run. In short, the West should have as its goal the formation of civil society, meaning respect for the rule of law, an independent judiciary, the principle that multiple political parties should be allowed to flourish and should not be suppressed regardless of who is in power, freedom of speech, property rights, minority rights, etc.[35] Without these underpinnings, democracy becomes the tyranny of the majority, and winner takes all. This is what would probably happen in Algeria if the Islamic Salvation Front takes power. Civil society is a necessary precondition of a fully functional liberal democracy. In Egypt, Algeria and elsewhere, existing regimes should be urged to reform and open up their legal systems, allow greater dialogue with opposition parties, permit greater freedom of speech and of the press, allow minority groups and others to demonstrate and petition the government (on women's rights issues for example) without risking being beaten, arrested or attacked by police or fundamentalist thugs. These steps will pave the way for a democratic system that can endure over time and that is truly worthy of our support.

VIII. Postscript

As this volume goes to press, Turkey's two old-line political parties, outgoing Turkish prime minister Tansu Ciller's True Path and the center-right Motherland Party, are attempting to prevent the rise to power of the Islamic fundamentalist Welfare (Refah) Party which captured a surprising 158 seats in the expanded 550 member parliament in national elections held on December 24, 1995[36]. The Welfare Party won a shocking 21.4 percent of the vote, more than any other political party in Turkey[37]. In comparison, Motherland and True Path won 19.7 and 19.2 percent of the vote each[38]. It must now be conceded that the fundamentalists are as effective at the ballot box as any other major political movement. They can no longer be discounted as marginal political players, even in such relatively affluent nations as Turkey.

Plainly, it is time for the Islamists to share power as the largest vote getter in the country. But True Path and Motherland are attempting to make peace with one another and strike a deal which would prevent the Welfare Party from obtaining the prime minister's chair or any seat in the cabinet. The ball is presently in President Suleyman Demirel's court. Although he is not technically bound under the Turkish constitution to ask Welfare to form a government[39], President Demirel may very well have to do so in light of their recent electoral success. American educated Tansu Ciller is clearly a lame duck at this point, a caretaker prime minister whose free market economics theories and Western-friendly policies have been affirmatively repudiated by Turkish citizens at the polls. Another general election is possible if the three dominant parties are incapable of forming some kind of coalition government.

Voting patterns in Turkey since at least 1991 have increasingly favored the traditional Muslims[40]. Judging from these voting trends, time is obviously on the fundamentalists' side. If, as expected, the Muslim fundamentalists eventually win control of Turkey, Welfare Party leader Mecmettin Erbakan has said he would "uncouple" Turkey from NATO and the West and move to create, among other things, a "union of Islamic states."[41]   Sound familiar?   Erbakan and other Islamists have also repeatedly discussed practising "Islamic economics" that would comply in all respects with the Koran's anti-usury provisions.

One may do well to ask: Why now?   Why should a regional or even hemispheric fundamentalist Muslim revolution succeed at this point in time when it didn't succeed in 1979 or 1980 upon the installation of the radical Muslims in Tehran, or at any time since?   Georgetown University Professor John Esposito has concluded from this fact that "there is no global Islamic [fundamentalist] threat."[42]   I disagree with Prof. Esposito for at least two reasons:

First, the Islamic Revolution has not spread until relatively recently because it has been undergoing a process of consolidation as the fundamentalist Muslims learned for the first time how to handle the levers of power and run a national government.   Now that the mullahs have trained a generation of ideologically committed party members to run various government agencies effectively on their own, the Islamic Revolution has begun in the last several years (and especially since the end of the Iran-Iraq War in 1988) to spread its tentacles outward.   As noted earlier, Iran has sought to make inroads in Central Asia and has reached out to provide covert aid to radical Muslims in other countries such as Algeria,

Saudi Arabia and Egypt. Tehran's ties to Sudan's Islamic regime are especially close.

More recently, Iran's influence has spread into southeastern Europe. Tehran has worked to forge strong ties to the fledgling Bosnian Government, going so far as to send several hundred to several thousand Revolutionary Guards and other soldiers (volunteers known as mujahedeen) to fight alongside the Bosnians[43]. Tehran also made clandestine arms shipments to Bosnia and has provided several hundred Bosnian soldiers with military training and Islamic revolutionary indoctrination back in Tehran[44]. After the Dayton Peace Accords ended the fighting in the former Yugoslavia, NATO peacekeeping troops discovered a terrorist training center run by Iranians located outside Sarajevo that contained educational materials for the teaching of bombmaking and kidnapping[45]. The Iranians associated with the facility were expelled but NATO officials suspect that many more remain under the guise of Iranian relief agency workers or as allegedly civilian "teachers."[46] Iran has also affirmatively sought out Bosnian officers and military commanders who are sympathetic to its brand of militant Islam and worked to advance the careers of these individuals[47]. According to news reports, NATO commanders in Bosnia were disturbed by the appointment in January, 1996 of Hasan Cengic to the post of Deputy Defense Minister[48]. Cengic spent most of his time during the Yugoslav war working closely with Iranian officials arranging for the shipment of arms and other supplies[49]. Perhaps most ominously, Iran has significantly increased its military spending since 1988 and seems absolutely determined to build an "Islamic Bomb." Its nuclear weapons program continues unabated.

Second, up until 1990-91 fundamentalist Islam was just one of several available political ideologies (and if fundamentalist Islam does not have a political dimension I don't know what does) competing for the hearts and minds of the populace in that region of the world. Thus, it was comparatively more difficult for political Islam to "break out" and compete successfully for the loyalties of the people in an already crowded ideological field. Added to this fact were the tremendous amounts of time and energy both the Western bloc and the Communist bloc spent trying to thwart each other in that region of the world. This too had the effect of dampening or thwarting political Islam's appeal.

Now that communism and to a lesser yet significant degree socialism have been definitively discredited with the end of the Cold War and the collapse of the Soviet Union and its communist empire in Eastern Europe, there are now only two major ideologies from which to choose: the Western ideology of democracy with its economic corollary capitalism, or Islam. In contrast to democracy which, like communism, is a relatively recent import from outside, Islam is an indigenous ideology with a 1400 year long track record in the region.

Muslims throughout Asia, North Africa and the Middle East are seeing that Westernization is not inevitable, that there is indeed another way to organize their society without capitulating to capitalism or Western material culture. Communism may be dead as a possible source of emulation. But Westernization and democracy need not be inevitable. There is a "Third Way" - Islam, which provides a complete prescription for living, both for the individual and for society. This is the fundamental political reality upon which Western historians and policymakers should set their sights.

§ § §

ENDNOTES

1.   Remarks of Cooper, "ACTIVE DEFENSE: How Can Allies and Friends and US Forward-Positioned Forces Be Protected Against Nuclear Attack?" Speech materials available from the American Security Council Foundation, Washington, D.C. Ambassador Cooper is currently a private consultant and Senior Associate of the National Institute for Public Policy and is the former Director of the Strategic Defense Initiative program and former Chief US Negotiator at the Geneva Defense and Space Talks with the Soviet Union. See also Remarks of Cooper, "COMMENTS ON BALLISTIC MISSILE DEFENSES."

2.   Testimony of Dr. Edward Teller, Defense Strategy Forum, Washington, D.C., September 21, 1993. The Defense Strategy Forum was convened by a group of prominent individuals from both major American political parties who came from military, scientific and civilian backgrounds and who vigorously opposed the Clinton Administration's deep defense

cuts as unwise and imprudent. A written copy of Dr. Teller's testimony was kindly made available to the author by the American Security Council Foundation.

3.   For a discussion of American Cold War defense strategy, see Gaddis, *Strategies Of Containment: A Critical Appraisal of Postwar American National Security Policy*. Gaddis provides a detailed account of America's defense policy during the Cold War years and analyzes the differences and similarities between each successive American Administration in this regard. For an analysis of the Cold War generally, see Ulam, *The Rivals: America & Russia Since World War II*. Prof. Ulam provides substantial insights into the psychology and motives of Soviet leaders such as Stalin.

4.   Kennan, "The Sources of Soviet Conduct."

5.   For an analysis of the People's Republic of China's burgeoning nuclear missile capabilities, see Asian Studies Center, "BUILDING A MORE SECURE ASIA THROUGH MISSILE DEFENSE," *Backgrounder*, No. 138 (October 24, 1995).

6.   Keith B. Payne, "Ballistic Missile Proliferation - An Audit," *Jane's Intelligence Review Yearbook*, (1994); Senate Select Committee on Intelligence, "Senate Intelligence Committee Releases Unclassified Intelligence Assessments,' *News Release*, 1 (May 1, 1995).

7.   Remarks of David Kay, Testimony before the Senate Committee on Foreign Relations, *Senate Hearing*, 102-422, available in *Nuclear Proliferation: Learning from the Iraq Experience*, 20.

8.   Missile Defense Study Team, "DEFENDING AMERICA," 12, footnote 17 (1995).

9.   Ibid.

10.   Remarks of Cooper, "ACTIVE DEFENSE."

11.   "The threat from space," *The Economist*, 13 (September 11-17, 1993).

12.   Report of the International Study Group on Proliferation and Missile Defenses, "Proliferation and Missile Defense: European-Allied and Israeli Perspectives."

13.   Parkhomenko, "Marshall Shaposhnikov: 'Russian President's Statements Are Political Statements...' Commander in Chief of CIS Combined Forces Answers *Nezavisimaya Gazeta* Correspondent's Questions," *Nezavisimaya Gazeta*, 2 (February 12, 1992), in *FBIS, Daily Report: Central Eurasia*, 1-2 (February 12, 1992).

14.   Kirkpatrick, "'Outlaw' states make ballistic missile defense a must," 25.

15.   Comments of Cooper, "COMMENTS ON BALLISTIC MISSILE DEFENSES."

16.   For the history of the Manhattan Project and the development of the A-bomb, see Sherwin, *A World Destroyed: The Atom Bomb and the Grand Alliance*.

17.   *Aviation Week*, February 11, 1991.

18.   For a history of the SDI program through all its permutations over the years, see Reiss, *The Strategic Defense Initiative*.

19.   Comments of Cooper, "ACTIVE DEFENSE." For a good, single source discussion of possible forms of missile defense, their associated costs and technological feasibility, see Missile Defense Study Team, *DEFENDING AMERICA: A Near- and Long-Term Plan to Deploy Missile Defenses*. This report advocates deployment of global missile defenses, first by sea, using the Navy's existing Upper Tier program, and then in space. The sea-based system is both cheaper and more capable than land-based missile defense systems. Protection would initially be limited to the continental U.S. and Europe. The study team was composed of former senior U.S. military and civilian officials who believe effective missile defenses are being given short shrift by the Clinton Administration with potentially catastrophic consequences for U.S. citizens. The group's final report criticizes the Clinton Administration for, among other missteps, shelving available anti-missile technologies in a "misguided effort

to 'dumb down' theater defenses for U.S. troops, friends, and allies." *Ibid.* at 47.

20.   William McFarlane op-ed article, *The New York Times* (August 24, 1993); Missile Defense Study Team, *DEFENDING AMERICA*, 43, 44.

21.   "President Boris Yeltsin's Statement on Arms Control," *TASS* (January 29, 1992). President Yeltsin reiterated his historic offer to the U.S. in a speech before the United Nations Security Council. United Nations Security Council, "Provisional Verbatim Record of the Three Thousand and Forty-sixth Meeting," S/PV.3046 p. 44 (January 31, 1992).

22.   Payne, Vlahos, Stanley, "EVOLVING RUSSIAN VIEWS ON DEFENSE: AN OPPORTUNITY FOR COOPERATION," 61-72.

23.   Missile Defense Study Team, *Defending America*, 31.

24.   Ibid.

25.   Ibid. at 30-32.

26.   Ibid. at 31.

27.   The Defense Strategy Forum was held in Room 2226 of the Rayburn House Office Building, Washington, D.C. on Tuesday, September 21, 1993. For an analysis of Clinton's military budget cuts and the deleterious impact those reductions are having on military readiness and capabilities, see Tonelson "Superpower Without a Sword," 166-180.

28.   Remarks of Cooper, "COMMENTS ON BALLISTIC MISSILE DEFENSES."

29.   Remarks of Cooper, "ACTIVE DEFENSE."

30.   Jeane Kirkpatrick, "'Outlaw' states make ballistic missile defense a must," *Journal Inquirer*, 25 (Wednesday, March 1, 1995).

31.   Mandelbaum, "Lessons of the Next Nuclear War," 33-37.

32. Ibid., 36.

33. Ibid., 32.

34. Miller, "The Challenge of Radical Islam," 45-46.

35. For a discussion of civil society and its relationship to liberty, see Gellner, *Conditions of Liberty: Civil Society and Its Rivals*; see also "SYMPOSIUM: Resurgent Islam in the Middle East," 8 (remarks of Dr. Daniel Pipes).

36. "Guess who will govern," *The Economist*, 39-40 (January 6-12, 1996).

37. Ibid.

38. Ibid.

39. Ibid. at 40.

40. Ibid. at 39.

41. Ibid. at 40.

42. "The Red Menace Is Gone. But Here's Islam," *The New York Times*, Week in Review (Section 4) 1, 6 (January 21, 1996).

43. "Bosnians Sending Soldiers To Iran To Get Training," *The New York Times*, A1, A6 (March 3, 1996).

44. Ibid.

45. Ibid.

46. Ibid.

47. Ibid. at A6.

48. Ibid.

49. Ibid.

BIBLIOGRAPHY

Books, Journals, Syndicated Columns and Reports:

Anderson, Jack "Headlines You Could See in 1994." *Parade Magazine* (December 26, 1993): 6.

Asian Studies Center. "BUILDING A MORE SECURE ASIA THROUGH MISSILE DEFENSE." *Backgrounder.* No. 138 (October 24, 1995).

Beschloss, Michael and Strobe Talbott *At The Highest Levels: The Inside Story Of The End Of The Cold War.* New York, N.Y.: Little, Brown and Company, 1993.

Bodansky, Yossef *TARGET AMERICA: Terrorism in the U.S. Today.* New York, N.Y.: S.P.I. Books, 1993.

----------------------- *TERROR! The Inside Story Of The Terrorist Conspiracy In America.* New York, N.Y.: S.P.I. Books, 1994.

Brooks, Geraldine *NINE PARTS DESIRE: The Hidden World of Islamic Women.* New York, N.Y.: Doubleday, 1975.

Collins, John M. "Transnational Terrorism And Counteractions: A Primer." *Congressional Research Service Report for Congress* (March 18, 1993).

Cooper, Henry F. "ACTIVE DEFENSES: How Can Allies and Friends and US Forward-Positioned Forces Be Protected Against Nuclear Attack?" *A Strategic Options Assessments Conference On Counter-Proliferation: Deterring Emerging Nuclear Actors* (July 7-8, 1993).

---------------------- "COMMENTS ON BALLISTIC MISSILE DEFENS-ES." *Republican Defense Policy Task Force* (August 25, 1993).

Davidson, James Dale and Lord William Rees-Mogg *The Great Reckoning: Protect Yourself in the Coming Depression*. New York, N.Y.: Touchstone, 1993.

Esposito, John L. *The Islamic Threat: Myth or Reality?* New York, N.Y.: Oxford University Press, 1992.

Famighetti, Robert et. al., eds. *The World Almanac and Book of Facts 1994*. Mahwah, N.J.: Funk & Wagnalls, 1994.

Federal Bureau of Investigation, Terrorist Research and Analytical Center, Counterterrorism Section, Intelligence Division "Terrorism in the United States 1982-1992." Washington, D.C.: Federal Bureau of Investigation, 1993.

Fisher, David E. *Fire and Ice: The Greenhouse Effect, Ozone Depletion and Nuclear Winter*. New York, N.Y.: Harper, 1990.

Follett, Ken *On Wings of Eagles*. New York, N.Y.: William Morrow and Company, Inc., 1983.

Fukuyama, Francis *The End of History and the Last Man*. New York, N.Y.: Simon & Schuster, 1991.

Gaddis, John Lewis *Strategies Of Containment: A Critical Appraisal of Postwar American National Security Policy*. New York, N.Y.: Oxford University Press, 1982.

Gellner, Ernest *CONDITIONS OF LIBERTY: Civil Society and Its Rivals*. New York, N.Y.: The Penguin Press, 1994.

Halliday, Fred "An Elusive Normalization: Western Europe And The Iranian Revolution." *Middle East Journal* 48, no. 2 (Spring 1994): 309-326.

Hersch, Seymour M. "The Wild East." *The Atlantic Monthly* (June 1994): 61-86.

Hopwood, Derek *Egypt: Politics and Society 1945-1981*. London, Great Britain: George Allen & Unwin Ltd., 1982.

150   Anthony J. Dennis

Hovsepian, Nubar "Competing Identities in the Arab World." *Journal of International Affairs* 49, no. 1 (Summer 1995): 1-24.

Hunter, Brian, ed. *The Statesman's Yearbook 1992-93.* New York, N.Y.: St. Martin's Press, 1992.

Hunter, Shireen *IRAN AND THE WORLD: Continuity in a Revolutionary Decade.* Bloomington, Ind.: Indiana University Press, 1990.

Huntington, Samuel P. "The Clash of Civilizations." *Foreign Affairs* 72, no 3 (Summer 1993): 22-49.

International Study Group on Proliferation and Missile Defenses "Proliferation and Missile Defense: European-Allied and Israeli Perspectives." Washington, D.C.: National Institute for Public Policy, June 1993.

Joffe, E.G.H. "Relations Between The Middle East And The West." *Middle East Journal* 48, no. 2 (Spring 1994): 250-267.

Jones, E.L. *The European Miracle: Environments, Economies and Geopolitics in the History of Europe and Asia.* New York, N.Y.: Cambridge University Press, 1981.

Kaplan, Robert D. "Shatter Zone." *The Atlantic Monthly* (April 1992): 24-34.

Kay, David "Testimony before the Senate Committee on Foreign Relations." *Senate Hearing.* 102-422 (1992).

Keddie, Nikki R. *Roots of Revolution: An Interpretive History of Modern Iran.* New Haven, CT.: Yale University Press, 1981.

Kennan, George "The Sources of Soviet Conduct." *Foreign Affairs* XXV (July 1947): 566-582.

Kennedy, Paul *The Rise And Fall Of The Great Powers.* New York, N.Y.: Random House, 1987.

Kepel, Gilles *MUSLIM EXTREMISM IN EGYPT: The Prophet And the Pharaoh*. Berkeley, CA: University of California Press, 1985.

Kirkpatrick, Jean "'Outlaw' states make ballistic missile defense a must." *Journal Inquirer* (March 1, 1995): 25.

Korany, Bahgat "Arab Democratization: A Poor Cousin?" *PS: POLITICAL SCIENCE & POLITICS* XXVII, no. 3 (September 1994): 511-513.

Kuniholm, Bruce R. "Turkey and the West." *Foreign Affairs* 70, no. 2 (Spring 1991): 34-48.

Kupperman, R. and J. Kamen *Final Warning*. New York, N.Y.: Doubleday, 1989.

LaFeber, Walter *America, Russia, and the Cold War: 1945-1980*. New York, N.Y.: John Wiley & Sons, 1980.

Laffin, J. *Holy War: Islam Fights*. London, Great Britain: Grafton Books, 1988.

Langewiesche, William "Turabi's Law." *The Atlantic Monthly* (August 1994): 26-33.

Lewis, Bernard *The Emergence of Modern Turkey*. New York, N.Y.: Oxford University Press, 2nd ed. 1967.

------------------ "Islam And Liberal Democracy." *The Atlantic Monthly* (February 1993): 89-98.

Locke, John, (J.W. Gough ed.) *A Letter concerning Toleration; with the Second Treatise of Civil Government*. New York, N.Y.: Oxford University Press, 1946.

MacDonough, Steve, ed. *The Rushdie Letters: Freedom to Speak, Freedom to Write*. Lincoln, Neb.: University of Nebraska Press, 1992.

Mahmoody, Betty with William Hoffer *NOT WITHOUT MY DAUGHTER*. New York, N.Y.: St. Martin's Press, 1987.

152   Anthony J. Dennis

Mandelbaum, Michael "Lessons of the Next Nuclear War." *Foreign Affairs* 74, no. 2 (March/April 1995): 22-37.

Marr, Phebe "The United States, Europe, And The Middle East: An Uneasy Triangle." *Middle East Journal* 48, no. 2 (Spring 1994): 211-225.

Mayer, Ann Elizabeth "Islam And The State." *Cardozo Law Review* 12 (1991): 1015-1056.

Miller, Judith "The Challenge of Radical Islam." *Foreign Affairs* 72, no. 2 (Spring 1993): 43-56.

Missile Defense Study Team *DEFENDING AMERICA: A Near- and Long-Term Plan to Deploy Missile Defenses.* Washington, D.C.: The Heritage Foundation, 1995.

Morganthau, Tom et. al. "The New Terrorism." *Newsweek* (July 5, 1993): 18-23.

Mortimer, Edward *Faith & Power: The Politics of Islam.* New York, N.Y.: Vintage Books, 1982.

Mostyn, Trevor et. al. eds. *The Cambridge Encyclopedia of the Middle East and North Africa.* New York, N.Y.: Cambridge University Press, 1988.

Nixon, Richard M. *SEIZE THE MOMENT: America's Challenge in A One-Superpower World.* New York, N.Y.: Simon & Schuster, 1992.

Office of Technology Assessment "Technology Against Terrorism: The Federal Effort." *OTA Report Brief* (July 1991) Washington, D.C.: Congressional Research Service, Library of Congress.

Olcott, Martha Brill "Central Asia's Catapult to Independence." *Foreign Affairs* 71, no. 3 (Summer 1993): 108-130.

Paul, John II *Crossing The Threshold Of Hope.* New York, N.Y.: Alfred Knopf, 1994.

Parkhomenko, Sergey "Marshall Shaposhnikov: 'Russian President's Statements Are Political Statements...' Commander in Chief of CIS Combined Forces Answers *Nezavisimaya Gazeta* Correspondent's Questions." *Nezavisimaya Gazeta* (February 12, 1992): 2.

Payne, Keith B. "Ballistic Missile Proliferation - An Audit." *Jane's Intelligence Review Yearbook.* 1994.

Payne, Keith B., Linda H. Vlahos and Willis A. Stanley "EVOLVING RUSSIAN VIEWS ON DEFENSE: AN OPPORTUNITY FOR COOPERATION." *STRATEGIC REVIEW* XXI, no. 1 (Winter 1993): 61-72.

Pfaff, William *THE WRATH OF NATIONS: Civilization And The Furies Of Nationalism.* New York, N.Y.: TOUCHSTONE, 1993.

Phillips, James A. "The Saddamization of Iran." *Policy Review* 69 (Summer 1994): 6-13.

Pipes, Daniel and Patrick Clawson "Ambitious Iran, Troubled Neighbors." *Foreign Affairs* 72, no. 1 (1992/93): 124-141.

Pope, Laurence "Department's Efforts To Combat International Terrorism." *US Department of State Dispatch* 4, no. 17 (April 26, 1993).

Ramazani, R.K. ed. *IRAN'S REVOLUTION: The Search for Consensus.* Bloomington, Ind.: Indiana University Press, 1990.

Reiss, Edward *The Strategic Defense Initiative.* New York, N.Y.: Cambridge University Press, 1992.

Revell, Oliver "Protecting America." *Middle East Quarterly* II, no. 1 (March 1995): 3-8.

Rushdie, Salman *The Satanic Verses.* New York, N.Y.: Viking, 1989.

---------------------- "One Thousand Days in a Balloon." *The Rushdie Letters: Freedom to Speak, Freedom to Write.* Steve Macdonough, ed. Lincoln, Neb.: University of Nebraska Press (1992): 15-24.

154   Anthony J. Dennis

Safran, Nadav *Israel: The Embattled Ally*. Cambridge, MA: Harvard University Press, 1981.

Sagan, Carl *A Path Where No Man Thought: Nuclear Winter and the End of the Arms Race*. New York, N.Y.: Random House, 1990.

Sahebjam, Freidoune *The Stoning of Soraya M*. New York, N.Y.: Arcade Publishing, 1994.

Sasson, Jean P. *PRINCESS: A True Story Of Life Behind The Veil In Saudi Arabia*. New York, N.Y.: AVON BOOKS, 1992.

Schapiro, Leonard *The Communist Party Of The Soviet Union*. New York, N.Y.: Vintage Books, 2nd ed. 1971.

Select Committee on Intelligence, U.S. Senate. "Senate Intelligence Committee Releases Unclassified Intelligence Assessments." *Senate Select Committee on Intelligence News Release*. (May 1, 1995).

Shaw, Stanford and Ezel Kural Shaw *History of the Ottoman Empire and Modern Turkey, Volume II: Reform, Revolution and Republic: The Rise of Modern Turkey 1808-1975*. New York, N.Y.: Cambridge University Press, 1977.

Sherwin, Martin *A World Destroyed: The Atom Bomb and the Grand Alliance*. New York, N.Y.: Vintage Books, 1977.

Sick, Gary "Iran: The Adolescent Revolution." *Journal of International Affairs* 49, no. 1 (Summer 1995): 145-166.

Sivan, Emmanuel "Eavesdropping on Radical Islam." *Middle East Quarterly* II, no. 1 (March 1995): 13-24.

State Department "Patterns of Global Terrorism: 1992." Washington, D.C.: U.S. Government Printing Office, 1993.

SYMPOSIUM "Resurgent Islam in the Middle East." *Middle East Policy* III, no. 2 (1994): 1-21.

Taheri, Amir *Cresent in a Red Sky: The Future Of Islam In The Soviet Union*. London, Great Britain: Hutchinson & Co. Ltd., 1989.

Teller, Dr. Edward "Testimony of Dr. Edward Teller." *Defense Strategy Forum* (September 21, 1993).

Terry, Sara "Drinking Water Comes to a Boil." *The New York Times Magazine* (September 26, 1993): 45.

Tonelson, Alan "Superpower Without a Sword." *Foreign Affairs* 72, no. 3 (Summer 1993): 166-180.

Ulam, Adam B. *The Rivals: America and Russia Since World War II*. New York, N.Y.: Penguin Books, 1971.

United Nations, Department of Economic and Social Information and Policy Analysis *World Economic and Social Survey 1994: Current Trends and Policies in the World Economy*. New York, N.Y.: United Nations Printing Office, 1994.

Vasiliev, A.A. *History of the Byzantine Empire*. (2 vols.) Madison, WI: University of Wisconsin Press, 2nd ed. 1952.

Waller, Douglas "Counterterrorism: Victim of Success?" *Newsweek* (July 5, 1993): 22-23.

Weiss, Bernard G. and Arnold H. Green *A Survey of Arab History*. Cairo, Egypt: The American University of Cairo Press, 1987.

Wootten, James P. "Terrorism: U.S. Policy Options." *Congressional Research Service Issue Brief* (July 22, 1993).

Winkler, Karen J. "Islam and Democracy." *The Chronicle of Higher Education* (October 5, 1994): A10.

Wright, Robin, *SACRED RAGE: The Wrath of Militant Islam*. New York, N.Y.: Simon & Schuster, 1985.

------------------, "Islam, Democracy and the West," *Foreign Affairs* 71, no. 3 (Summer 1992): 131-145.

Yeats, William Butler, "The Second Coming." *Selected Poems And Two Plays*. (M.L. Rosenthal ed.) New York, N.Y.: Collier Books, 1982.

Yergin, Daniel *The Prize: The Epic Quest For Oil, Money & Power*. New York, N.Y.: Simon & Schuster, 1991.

United Nations Documents:

International Covenant on Civil and Political Rights, United Nations General Assembly Resolution 2200 (XXI), 21 U.N. GAOR, Supp. (No. 16) 52 U.N. Doc. A/6316 (1967), reprinted in 6 I.L.M. 368 (1967).

United Nations Security Council, "Provisional Verbatim Record of the Three Thousand and Forty-sixth Meeting," S/PV.3046 p. 44 (January 31, 1992).

Universal Declaration of Human Rights, Dec. 10, 1948, United Nations General Assembly Resolution 217 A (III), U.N. Doc. A/810, at 71 (1948).

Newspapers: As cited in the Endnotes.

ABOUT THE AUTHOR

A recognized expert on terrorism and Islamic fundamentalism, Anthony J. Dennis's views are regularly and eagerly sought by the media. He has been a guest on well over one hundred syndicated talk radio and television news programs over the past several years. His writings on these and related topics have appeared in a variety of publications both in the U.S. and abroad including *The Hartford Courant, The Maccabean, The Wall Street Journal, The Washington Times*, the public policy journal *NATIV*, and *FIRST THINGS* magazine.

Immediately following the September 11th attacks, Mr. Dennis was approached by the media and his views concerning the terrorist threat were extensively quoted by The New York Post in several articles.

In addition to authoring the present volume, Mr. Dennis also served as editor and a principal contributor of the historic and unprecedented book of letters and essays entitled *"Letters to Khatami: A Reply to the Iranian President's Call for a Dialogue Among Civilizations"* (Wyndham Hall Press, 2001).

Mr. Dennis is an independent scholar living in the United States. He holds degrees in law, literature and history from Northwestern University School of Law and Tufts University.